A CRITIQUE OF
FREEDOM AND EQUALITY

Cambridge Studies in the History and Theory of Politics

A CRITIQUE OF
FREEDOM AND EQUALITY

JOHN CHARVET

Reader in Political Science at the
London School of Economics and Political Science

CAMBRIDGE UNIVERSITY PRESS

Cambridge
London   New York   New Rochelle
Melbourne   Sydney

Published by the Press Syndicate of the University of Cambridge
The Pitt Building, Trumpington Street, Cambridge CB2 IRP
32 East 57th Street, New York, NY 10022, USA
296 Beaconsfield Parade, Middle Park, Melbourne 3206, Australia

First published 1981

Printed in Great Britain by
Western Printing Services Ltd, Bristol

British Library Cataloguing in Publication Data
Charvet, John
A critique of freedom and equality.
– (Cambridge studies in the history and theory
of politics)
1. Liberty
I. Title
323.44'01   HM271   80–42087
ISBN 0 521 23727 0

CONTENTS

	page
Acknowledgements	vii
Introduction	1
Part I	11
The equal value of individuals as self-determining beings	11
A preliminary notice of the difficulties	19
Authenticity	21
Egoism	23
The principle of equal value in some contemporary literature	25
The motivational structure of morality	38
Hobbesian egoism	41
Benevolence and sympathy	51
Rousseau	55
Rationalism and Kant	69
Self-interest, morality and the divided self	81
Utilitarianism	86
Subordinate ordering principles	95
The liberal theory of equal freedom	96
Egalitarianism	102
The Rawlsian combination	109
Part II	117
Hegel	117
Marx	135

Contents

Part III   157

The relativity of value   157
The fundamental moral attitude   161
The possibility of morality   163
The moral attitude and the rights of individuals   165
The right to particular satisfaction or welfare   171
The standpoint of the whole   172
Ethical criticism   193
Subjectivity and objectivity in morals   196
The unity of the human race   199

Index   201

ACKNOWLEDGEMENTS

I am very grateful to my friends and colleagues, Shirley Letwin, Michael Oakeshott, Richard Flathman and Christopher Cherry, and to my sister, Anne Charvet, for their kindness in giving their time and judgement to improving the content or style of this work. I am above all grateful to my wife, Barbara Charvet, for her critical interest in, and encouragement of, my ideas over many years, as well as for her special attention to their presentation in this book.

INTRODUCTION

In this work ideas of human freedom and equality are understood to be integral expressions of the dominant modern conception of the basis of moral and political life. The aim of the work is in the first place to show that the notions of freedom and equality must be taken together in the idea of the equal value of individuals as free or self-determining beings, and yet that this necessary combination of equality and freedom cannot be elaborated into a coherent system of ethical thought. The principles of freedom and equality are as much opposed to each other as they require each other. From this I conclude that they cannot be the *fundamental* principles in terms of which we can account adequately for our ethical experience. Part I is thus a critical and negative argument.

In Part II I consider the views of two major theorists who also reject individualist conceptions of freedom and equality, Hegel and Marx. My concern is to show how their accounts of the basis of moral experience, while doing justice to its communal nature, fail to leave an adequate place for the particular individual. In Part III I offer my own account of how the basis of our ethical experience is to be construed. This account, while rejecting the individualist position, will be seen both to owe much to it and to give a more determinate and coherent explanation for many of the moral and political practices associated with that position. Crudely, not individuals but men's associated wills in community constitute the basis of our ethical experience. But since everything in this account depends on how community is to be understood, and since my understanding of it can be grasped only in relation to what emerges from my critique of individualism, I will not now say anything further to illuminate this claim.

I emphasize that I am here primarily concerned with freedom

and equality in so far as they are fundamental principles, or integral expression of principles, that account for our moral experience. By a fundamental principle I mean one that explains our sense of moral obligation, our sense of being bound in the first place to restrict the pursuit of our particular interests by respect for principles or rules, as a result of which others are benefited. Our basic moral experience consists in the recognition that there is an order of some kind to which we must conform our particular desires if these desires are to have legitimacy. A fundamental principle gives the source of that legitimacy-bestowing order or is the first principle of that order. It explains the existence of our moral obligations by constituting the ground of moral value in the world.

On some ethical views God's will functions as such a fundamental principle. In so far as the individual conforms his will to God's will and to the order which that will expresses, his actions, even those directed towards his particular interests, have moral worth. Here the source of moral worth lies outside human beings in a divine principle, although men participate in it in so far as they can grasp the principle and direct themselves in accordance with it. Indeed a general characteristic of pre-modern ethical views is that the source of moral worth is located in some meta-human principle, whereas the general characteristic of modern views is that this source is to be found in man himself. The notions of freedom and equality are so important to the modern world, because they are taken to be necessary expressions of this idea. This, I shall argue, is a mistake. Freedom and equality are necessary expressions of the idea that man himself is the source of moral worth only if man is understood as the individual man, rather than as men in their relations with each other.

In pre-modern ethical views, as it is frequently noticed, men have duties and not rights. This is because the source of moral worth lies outside the individual; hence the obligation on men to conform their wills to the source of value is not owed to other men, but to something divine and external to them. One is required to help or not to injure another, not for his sake, because he has value in himself, but for God's sake, and for one's own, in so far as on pre-modern views the condition of a well-ordered soul is its harmony with the divine principle. With the shift to a moral order centred on the individual man, rights also move to the centre of our moral experience, because they express the claim of individuals on each other to be a source of moral worth. In modern views men, of course, have duties in so far as they have rights, and duty may even appear to be the primary notion, as in Kant's theory. However, duty for Kant is not owed to some external principle but is an expression of the fact that man himself, as a rational being, is the source of moral worth; hence duty turns back on itself and must be done for its own sake. The obligation on man is to respect the value inherent in himself, and thus to respect the right residing in him.

I must briefly mention here two obvious objections to this simple characterization of the modern ethical idea in relation to the pre-modern. Firstly, one major modern ethical view is Utilitarianism, which, it may be thought, does not employ notions of freedom and equality other than in an empirical and subordinate role, or give prominence to the notion of rights. I shall discuss later the relation of Utilitarianism to ideas of freedom and equality.[1] Here I shall limit myself to affirming, what I there argue, that Utilitarianism either presupposes a notion of human rights tied to ideas of freedom and equality, which it does not make explicit, and so thinks that it does not employ, or, in clearly freeing itself from dependence on all such notions, is the morally unpleasant theory it is frequently attacked for being.

Secondly, much ethical writing of the early modern period especially, while proclaiming the rights of man and his natural freedom and equality, nevertheless retains the idea of God as the ultimate creator of and sanction for this moral order: for example, Locke in the *Second Treatise of Government*. On the basis of the above characterization of the modern ethical idea this combination appears to be a contradiction. If the moral

---

[1] See pp. 86–95 below.

3

order is grounded in God's will, then it would seem that men cannot have rights as men, but only as participants in that order; while, if they have rights as men, man himself must be the ground of the moral order.

But this opposition depends on an ambiguity in the idea of men having rights as men. Thus on the Lockeian view it is individuals as such, that is individuals in respect of their undifferentiated nature as men, who have rights and who are said to be free and equal. However, they have such rights not because of the value inherent in them as free beings but because God as the creator of value bestows it on them. The Lockeian position thus combines modern individualist elements expressed in terms of notions of freedom and equality with the pre-modern foundation of the moral order in a meta-human principle. This appeal to a meta-human ground limits the individualism of the theory and the fundamental nature of the freedom and equality in which it is expressed. The individualism of modern theories, which I shall be primarily concerned with, affirms both that men have equal rights as men *and* that the source of such rights lies in the individual himself. Individualism is thus not a wholly modern conception; nevertheless the modern form of it by removing the non-individualist divine ground of individual value is that much more extreme and unlimited.[2]

The fundamental principle, I said, accounts for our sense of being obliged to regulate the pursuit of our particular desires or interests so as to conform with the requirements of the moral order by giving us the ultimate ground of that order. To do this adequately, we need to know not simply what the ultimate ground is, but what our relation to it is; why as particular beings we should order our interests not by reference to our-

[2] These claims about modern ethical theories should be taken broadly. I do not mean, of course, that all ethical writing in the modern period is unambiguously both non-transcendental and individualist in character. Modern individualism as identified above is my primary target. The recognition of the need to make some such qualifications as are to be found in this paragraph I owe to the criticisms of earlier drafts by Shirley Letwin and Richard Flathman.

selves alone, but by reference to that ground and to the order founded on it. This presupposes that our particular life can and must be seen, *in the first instance*, as independent of the moral order. Were this not so, no philosophical problem about morality could possibly arise: it would be obvious in thinking about our particular life that it is related to a definite moral order, and it would be self-evidently absurd to distinguish that particular life from the order, as though the particular individual could have any value in himself apart from the order. The traditional philosophical problems of morality and politics are incomprehensible of they are not seen to involve the attempt to show how it is the particular individual's interest to conform his life to the moral order, an attempt to show why one should be moral.³ This is a central question in the opening of the first masterpiece of ethical thought in the West, and any 'philosophy', which seeks to show, or worse still assumes, that this is not a genuine question, is really seeking to abolish, or has in fact simply abandoned, philosophy in this field.⁴

This is not to say that the initial independence of the particular individual from the moral order is ultimately sustainable. Indeed the condition of a satisfactory answer to the problem of why one should be moral is that the particular individual be shown not to be ultimately independent of the ground of order, but to be himself constituted by the ground. In pre-modern theories the meta-human divine ground must be capable of being seen as the central element in the individual's own life, so that he is in harmony with himself only in so far as his particular life is being governed by the divine principle in him. His initial independence is an alienation of himself from his essence. This understanding of the individual's relation to the moral order can be achieved, however, only by proceeding through the 'original sin' of separating the particular individual

---

³ I do not mean by this that a moral justification must be given for being moral – an absurdity.

⁴ The fact that the tradition of Western moral philosophy originates with this question, which involves the initial separation of the individual from his moral community, and is thus individualist in nature, is another reason for not identifying individualism wholly with modernity.

from his ground and setting him up on his own in the pride of his claim to be himself the ground of order for his life.

I shall be concerned with this issue in the form in which it arises in modern theories where the ground of moral order is sought in man himself. In these theories, since the ground is not intended to be a meta-human one, the demonstration of the relation of the particular self to its ground would seem to require a relation that is wholly internal to the individual himself. I shall explore various attempts within modern theory to show how this is possible, and seek the reasons for their failure before proceeding to my own answer.

The initial alienation of the particular individual from his order involves his taking up what I shall call the independent standpoint. By this standpoint I mean simply that from it the individual conceives himself as the sole ground of order, and hence orders his life by reference to himself alone. I do not mean that in taking up the independent standpoint the individual becomes an isolated being and *actually* lives his life solely by reference to himself. I mean that from the independent standpoint this attitude is the only one that appears immediately justifiable. It is a separation in *thought* from others, even if the individual continues in his daily life to comply with the requirements of his community. Once the independent standpoint has been adopted in thought, the philosophical problem of an order that re-integrates the particular individual with others is raised.

The notion of the independent standpoint requires that the individual be a free agent, capable of having a conception of his life as a whole, of choosing ends to be pursued in it, and of directing himself in accordance with such ends. Although desires and impulses naturally arise in him, they do not immediately determine him, but he forms these desires into a system of ends for his life. Through his thought, he determines himself. I shall attempt neither to explore the presuppositions of this conception of human personality, nor to justify the individual's capacity for freedom against deterministic claims. I assume simply that man is a free, purposive agent, and concern myself with the ethical consequences of this assumption. This explains why the primary object of my criticism in Part I are those theories which make similar assumptions, and hence attach primary importance to men's rights expressed in terms of their claims to freedom and equality, and not anti-rights Utilitarian theories. I share with the theories I criticize the conception of man as a free being, and am thus relatively cavalier in my treatment of Utilitarianism in so far as it is to be understood as rejecting such a conception of man.

I must acknowledge here my awareness that the theories, which I shall be considering, do not all have the same conception of human freedom, and that this difference affects the way in which the values of freedom and equality are supported or elaborated in them. Broadly, there are, on the one hand, those conceptions of freedom which locate it simply in man's capacity to submit the desires and impulses that arise naturally in him to a process of mental deliberation, as a result of which he chooses to pursue this or that desire; and, on the other hand, those conceptions which claim that the central controlling agency, the self, must be independent of natural desire in a more radical way than is envisaged in the first conception. The distinction is between a view such as Hobbes's and a view such as Kant's. Both views, however, are used in individualist conceptions of freedom and equality, and my critique is aimed at encompassing both. The differences between them will, I hope, be sufficiently clear in the course of my argument.

If man is a free, purposive agent, then the independent standpoint is implicit in this capacity. In forming a conception of his life by choosing ends for himself to pursue in it, he necessarily takes himself to be the ground of value for his life, and orders his life by reference to himself. This is because in so far as *he* determines what ends to pursue, the values in his life are those determined by himself. The fact that he has chosen them establishes their worth for him. The development of his free agency demands, then, that *he* and not something external to himself, nature or other men, determine his values. Thus the pressures and demands of society, if simply accepted by the individual without thought, would involve his life being formed by external forces. In developing his capacity for freedom, the individual must be able to come to see his relation to his society as a relation to external forces. It is this alienation of the self from its immediate relation to a moral order which constitutes the adoption of the independent standpoint. At the moment at which society appears external to him, he sees himself, in the first instance, as the sole ground of order in his life. From this point he must seek a way of relating himself to others again that overcomes their externality.

I said above that I am not supposing that men live from or in the independent standpoint. To suppose so would be to suppose men pursuing their ends without accepting that others had any claims on them at all. Even if there do exist 'egoistic' ethical theories, egoism is a pathological condition and could not be generally true of a society. The independent standpoint is one from which we do not see *how* others have any claims on us. It raises a theoretical question which can be relatively detached from our practical life, for we can continue to fulfil our existing obligations as a temporary measure, while not seeing how they can be justified. One contemplates one's life and one's relations to others from that standpoint and can thus consider in principle the character of the choices that would be made, if one were to live from it.

The independent standpoint is similar to the notion of the original position in Rawls's theory,[5] and to the state of nature in early modern theories, at least in so far as the state of nature is conceived in Hobbesian fashion as a state in which men do not have obligations to others, and not in Lockeian fashion as a state in which men do have such obligations. The original position according to Rawls is occupied by men who are purely self-interested,[6] but who seek principles for determining the division of social advantages. Rawls's conception of the original position thus contains the notion of the unproblematic nature of the pursuit by the individual of his own interests and the prob-

---

[5] J. Rawls, *A Theory of Justice*, Clarendon Press, 1971.
[6] They are not interested in each other's interests.

lematic nature of other-interested rationality. The former is given, while it is the nature and content of the latter that has to be established.

Rawls emphasizes the hypothetical nature of the original position and of the consequent contract which establishes the principles of justice; and by the notion of the veil of ignorance, which obliterates the individual's knowledge of his own and others' *particular* characteristics, leaving only a general knowledge of individuals and society, he emphasizes also the highly abstract self-conception which is involved in this idea. I take it that by these emphases Rawls means that one can always put oneself *in thought* into the original position by abstracting oneself from one's particular obligations, and conceiving one's individual nature in a highly general way. Of course, for Rawls it is not simply that one can do so; one must do so, in order to understand the nature and content of one's ethical relations to others. This is exactly my conception of the function of the independent standpoint. It is a necessary element in the derivation of an ethical understanding.

It is obvious, provided one treats the notion of the state of nature, or natural condition of mankind, in theorists such as Hobbes not as an actual state of particular life, but as a way of raising in thought general questions about the nature of one's individuality and its relation to others, that the notion contains the same idea as that expressed by Rawls in the concept of the original position, and by my concept of the independent standpoint. But the idea of the independent standpoint is contained in any argument that even touches upon the question of the justification of the claims others make on the individual, as we shall see in the cases to be considered in Part I.

Part I

CRICKDICKDICKDICKDICKDICKDICKDICKDICKDICKDICKDICKDICKDICKDICKDICKDICKDICKDICKDICKDICKDICKDICKDIC

THE EQUAL VALUE OF INDIVIDUALS
AS SELF-DETERMINING BEINGS

The modern moral idea holds or presumes that the source of moral value lies in human beings themselves and not in some meta-human principle. The importance of the notions of freedom and equality in modern ethical thought consists in their being a joint principle expressing this idea in a particular form, a form which understands the value of human beings to reside in each individual as such. The joint principle affirms the equal value of all men as self-determining beings, that is to say their equal value in respect of their being choosers of the particular ends they pursue in their lives.

By the *source* of moral worth here is meant that principle which bestows moral legitimacy on the particular choices and actions of individuals. Individuals are presumed to be, as already indicated, self-forming beings, in that they choose particular ends to pursue in their lives. Thus the notion that the individual himself is the source of the legitimacy of his own particular choices for his life means that by virtue of his making such choices he bestows at least prima facie[1] moral worth upon them. His worth consists in his self-determining capacity, or his freedom. The position involves then a distinction between the particular individual, the individual in respect of the actual choices he makes for his life, and the individual in respect of his pure capacity to make such choices.

By moral value or worth here I mean an objective and not a subjective value, a value for anyone and not just a value for the

---

[1] Since the particular choices of individuals are bound not to harmonize spontaneously, principles are required for resolving such conflicts. By the term prima facie I point to this requirement which will be taken up later.

particular individual, the worth of whose choices and actions are in question. To say that each individual has equal moral worth as a self-determining being is to say that each man's particular choices for his life are prima facie objective values, or values for anyone.

Notions of freedom and equality as expressive of primary principles involve the idea that men have fundamental rights as men, viz. natural or human rights, the rights of man. Certainly, if men have equal value as self-determining beings, then they must have a basic equal right to determine themselves, or an equal right to freedom. Affirmations of human rights, I shall claim, leaving aside the Lockeian equivocation, and the utilitarian thesis to be considered later, presuppose that the ground in which the right-bestowing value is rooted is the individual himself, and the value of the individual must consist in his free nature. Of course, we often find human rights affirmed without any backing at all.[2] But one cannot claim that nothing is presupposed in such proclamations. If human rights are not specifically derived from some other principle, the value that rights protect must be assumed to lie in the individual himself.

To support the above claims as to the content of the position that I shall be criticizing, I need to show that freedom and equality are necessarily connected in expressing the value inherent in individuals (if such value exists), and that views of the basic content of human rights that appear to reject freedom for something else, the satisfaction of needs, happiness, life, cannot in fact coherently do so, but must rest on the more fundamental right to freedom.

If there are basic rights other than the right to freedom, these rights will nevertheless be equal ones, and hence equality will be a primary value not necessarily connected to freedom. Let us consider first, then, whether the value of freedom can be expressed without its necessary connection with equality.

Suppose we say that the fundamental expression of the value of individuals lies in the right to freedom. We see immediately

[2] As in R. Nozick, *Anarchy, State and Utopia*, Basil Blackwell, 1974, p. ix.

that this must be an equal right of individuals as such. For if an individual has such a right by virtue of his individuality alone, then it must be the case that every such individual has the same right. If we claimed that a right to freedom was possessed by men only in respect of their having particular qualities or characteristics, for example being members of the Aryan race, or by virtue of the particular content of their choices, for example the pursuit of art or perfection, then, firstly, we are obviously no longer attributing the right to the individual as such, and secondly it is not a right to freedom that we are defending, but rather a right to pursue the interests of the Aryan race, or a right to the pursuit of perfection. Only choices directed to such ends can claim a right not to be interfered with by others, since only they embody value. A right to freedom, that is a fundamental principle of value, cannot limit the choices of individuals by other values, for then these values are more fundamental than freedom.

Can equality be expressed as the fundamental principle apart from freedom? Dworkin evidently thinks so.[3] He argues, first of all, that there cannot be a general right to freedom, since such a right would involve one's being able to do whatever one wants without any restraint whatsoever, whereas it is obvious that men's wants conflict, and that it is necessary to restrict one man's liberty in order to defend another's. Laws are necessary to protect equality, and laws are inevitably restraints on liberty. This argument ignores the fact that, as shown above, a right to liberty must be an equal right, and that a consequence generally drawn from this equality is that one individual's right to liberty, i.e. to do what he wants, does not include the right to infringe another's liberty. There are indeed insoluble problems connected with the conflict of wants, as I shall show in my later argument. But it is too facile to dismiss the notion of a right to freedom without first developing it in the form of an equal right.

Dworkin's concern, in treating a general right to freedom as an absurd notion, is to separate out the principles of freedom

[3] R. Dworkin, *Taking Rights Seriously*, Duckworth, 1977, chs. 11–12.

and equality in order to claim that equality on its own is the fundamental principle, and freedom only a limited and derivative one. Dworkin's fundamental right, which I take to express the idea of the value of the individual, is the right to treatment as an equal, which he elaborates as a right to equal concern and respect in the political decisions regarding the distribution of goods and opportunities. This reference to government decisions distracts one from the main point. For it appears that governments have a prior right to the command of all resources that individuals could want in the pursuit of their ends, and that the question to be answered by the equality principle is how these goods are to be distributed. As nothing is said about where the right of the government to all things comes from, it is unclear whether or not it constitutes a more fundamental principle than that of equality. But these obscurities can be ignored. The important issue is, in virtue of what are we to accord equal concern and respect to individuals? Dworkin's answer is that firstly we accord equal concern to men as sufferers, and secondly equal respect to them as beings capable of forming and acting on intelligent conceptions of how their lives should be lived. It is immediately obvious that this last part is simply the idea of the equal value of individuals as choosers of their own lives, and hence as free beings. In this respect, Dworkin's equality principle is not distinct from the freedom principle at all, but is, unbeknown to him, an expression of the unity of the two principles. In the first part of his answer a new principle appears to be involved. But what that principle is, is far from clear. We could treat it as an expression of the positive interpretation of the requirements of equal respect for men as choosers of their own lives. The negative side of equal respect requires us not to prevent men from realizing their conception of their lives. The positive side would require us actively to help men in their attempt to realize their conceptions, and in so far as they suffer from the misfortunes of nature and the arrangements of men, to provide a remedy for these. Such help would, of course, have to be distributed by us (or the government) in accordance with the requirements of the principle of equal value.

This is the way I shall interpret other formulations of the content of basic rights attributed to man as an individual, which appear to be alternatives to the right to freedom. They are, in fact, expressions of the value individuals have as such, and since the rights are held to be equal rights, the value expressed is an equal value. Thus views of basic human rights which include a right to the satisfaction of one's needs, the right to happiness or the right to life, I shall treat as corollaries of the more fundamental principle of the equal value of men as self-determining beings. Firstly, the right to the satisfaction of one's needs. The concept of need, as Miller argues,[4] is tied to that of harm. A person's needs are to be defined in terms of what is necessary to the satisfaction of his real interests, so that the lack of the things necessary can be said to harm him. The content of the real interests of each individual is determined by that individual himself in terms of his choice of ends for his life. Even if we restrict the right to the satisfaction of basic needs only, the notion of basic will have to be given meaning in terms of those conditions, e.g. health, education, housing, which are necessary for an individual to develop his capacities as a self-forming being in the first place, and thereafter to be in a position to realize his plans for his life whatever they are. Thus the right to the satisfaction of needs, if there is such a right, presupposes the prior value of the individual as a self-determining being.

The right to happiness is hardly different from the fuller version of the right to the satisfaction of one's needs. Of course, happiness may be understood as a sum of pleasures and we may adopt a utilitarian conception of this right. But putting utilitarianism aside yet again, I shall here simply affirm that by happiness I mean a state of the individual dependent on his attaining or being on the way to attain the ends he has chosen for his life, assuming also that these ends are appropriate to his natural capacities.[5] Here again the right to happiness, if there is such a right, is derivative from the value that resides in the

[4] D. Miller, *Social Justice*, Clarendon Press, 1976, pp. 130–6.
[5] See for an account of this conception of happiness J. Rawls, *A Theory of Justice*, Clarendon Press, 1971, pp. 548–54.

individual as a self-determining being. The right would require us to help each other to attain our ends, and so to provide, as far as we are able, whatever is necessary for such attainment.[6]

As to the supposed basic right to life, we need to know whether this is a right attributable only to human beings or to living beings generally. In the former case the question would arise as to what it is about human beings that bestows a special value on their lives, and the obvious non-religious answer to this will be in terms of the value of individuals as self-determining beings. In the latter case, given that the basic right is not derivative from utility or the Divine Will, we would have to suppose that it protects a value whose source lies in the individual living thing. But since for the most part these living things are incapable of moral action, we would be supposing that moral value is inherent in a being that can have no conception of moral value. This is absurd.[7]

The above interpretation of the idea that individuals have rights to what can be called, in general, welfare, can be brought together in the following argument: if the rights to welfare are attributable to individuals as such, and are not derived from an external principle, then we must understand that the condition of the individual's welfare depends on the individual's own choice of ends, or on his self-determination. The individual may, of course, make errors in his judgement of what are appropriate means to his ends, and may also make mistakes as to what are appropriate ends for him to pursue, given his capacities and environment; nevertheless, although another could judge what is appropriate for him better than the individual himself, that other could not secure the individual's welfare by imposing those ends on him without obtaining his willing endorsement of the ends, and thereby his making them his own. If, on the contrary, we held that the welfare of the individual was quite

---

[6] I discuss the implication of these two rights at greater length on pp. 102–9 below.

[7] The absurdity of attributing rights to animals and things can be supported on the similar ground that the capacity for rights requires the ability to assert, demand or insist that one has rights. See on this R. Flathman, *The Practice of Rights*, Cambridge University Press, 1976, pp. 86–8.

independent of his will, and consisted in e.g. a sum of pleasures, that could be produced by strapping the individual on to a pleasure machine,[8] we would be holding that value resided in pleasure, and that individuals held rights only derivatively, being those arrangements necessary in order to maximize the quantity of pleasure. If rights to welfare are not so derived, and we must understand the individual's welfare to depend on his own choice of ends, then the basic principle of value cannot lie in the welfare, but in that which is its determining condition.[9]

In saying that a conception of human rights presupposes that the individual himself is their ground, one is not claiming that such rights exist in the world independently of their being recognized by men in communities. The *realization* of such rights, as also the *realization* of the value that is supposed to reside in individuals, must depend on the actualization of such rights and such value in men's relations. But this does not show that the ground of the rights is something other than the individual himself, namely the recognition of the community. If one were serious in this matter of recognition by the community, one would have to hold that the rights of individuals are not in fact primary, but grounded in the superior value residing in the community. If one is not prepared to take such a position, all one can mean by the dependence of rights on their recognition, is the self-evident claim that such rights cannot be given actuality, if no one recognizes them. But in recognizing them, one recognizes the inherent value that resides in individuals.

Lukes in his book *Individualism* tries to accommodate the

---

[8] See Smart's fantasy in B. Williams and J. J. C. Smart, *Utilitarianism. For and Against*, Cambridge University Press, 1973, pp. 18–20.

[9] Hart, in a well-known article, argues for a fundamental equal right to freedom as the presupposition of the notion of a moral right. But he assumes in this that moral rights are claims to interfere with the freedom of action of others to pursue their own ends. He does not consider that moral rights include rights to welfare. I do not want to deny that on the individualist view there can be rights to welfare, and hence a further argument is necessary on this point to establish as the fundamental principle an equal right to freedom. See H. L. A. Hart, 'Are there any natural rights?' *Philosophical Review*, vol. 64, 1955.

social moment in the realization of the value inherent in individuals, by distinguishing between individualist doctrines, that contain an abstract conception of the individual, and ones that replace the abstract individual by the concept of a person. The former notion is that of a being whose nature is fixed independently of society, from which it is supposed to follow that society is merely the means for the individual to realize his independent ends.[10] Lukes holds that this does not treat the individual seriously as either a free or a social being. The person, however, is the individual understood as a self-determining being in terms similar to my own, and this apparently enables us to see him not as given outside society, but as developing his individuality in relation to a social order.[11]

The individuality so developed in relation to a social order is nevertheless for Lukes the capacity of the individual to form himself, and the values that Lukes affirms in respect of this capacity are the values residing in men as such self-forming beings expressed through the notions of freedom and equality. The fact that the individual develops this capacity in the first place as part of a social order does not mean that the social order creates the value of the individual in the sense of being the moral ground of it. The value of the self-forming individual must reside quite apart from the social order and in the individual himself. It is this value which the social order must recognize if it is to be a morally acceptable one. In this sense the social order exists morally in order to realize the value inherent in individuals. And as it is the individual as pure, self-forming being that has this value, it is the abstract individual, the individual in respect of his transcendence of his social order, who is the real basis of Lukes's supposedly concrete idea of the person. If individualist values are primary, then individuals in themselves, and not in their relations, are their root.

The view that men have equal value as self-determining beings might be thought to exclude the possibility of the indepen-

[10] S. Lukes, *Individualism*, Basil Blackwell, 1973, pp. 73–8.
[11] ibid., pp. 146–57.

dent standpoint, which, I claimed in the introduction, must be the implicit starting-point of any ethical theory. From the independent standpoint the individual, although seeing himself as a self-forming being, allows himself to be only a subjective value, or treats the ends that he would choose from that standpoint not as values for anyone, but as values only for himself. But the above position affirms that the individual as chooser of his life is of objective value. On this view it would seem impossible for the individual to conceive of himself as a chooser of his own life without conceiving of himself as having in that respect objective worth. In fact, much modern ethical argument, especially all rationalist arguments, are committed to showing that the objective position is necessarily contained within the conception of the individual as self-forming being, and hence that the subjective position cannot be coherently formulated. It is inherently unstable, moving by the force of the reason in it into the objective position. These arguments will be examined later. But we need only note here that such arguments still accept the necessity of showing that the objective position is contained within the subjective one, and thus accept that an initial plausibility is attached to the subjective position as a starting-point for ethical argument. Given that the objective position requires the idea of man as capable of making choices for his own life, the possibility of raising the question from the independent standpoint of why the individual should accept that value resides in others besides himself is always present.

A PRELIMINARY NOTICE OF THE DIFFICULTIES

The individualist ethical theory that I shall be criticizing, holds, on my view of it, that men in respect of their capacity as self-forming beings have objective moral worth. This value is bestowed by them on their particular lives in so far as these lives are self-chosen ones, or, in other words, embodiments of the capacity. One difficulty that such a theory involves is immediately obvious: the problem of conflict between the particular choices of different individuals. Such conflict is bound to occur. It is the reason that Dworkin gives, as we have seen, for rejecting the idea of a general right to freedom. But as the objection applies equally to his own view of what is man's fundamental right, his objection is self-defeating. The standard non-utilitarian way of attempting to deal with this problem is to seek objectively valid secondary principles which will further delimit the validity of particular choices. By judging only those choices to be valid that are compatible with the principles, the aim is to make all valid choices compatible with each other. To be objective principles, they must be interpretations of the primary principle of the equal value of individuals as self-forming beings, a principle which for the most part I shall hereafter call the principle of equal freedom. There are a number of alternative interpretations of the primary principle, which are offered as the objectively valid secondary principles, and I shall consider their broad structure and satisfactoriness towards the end of Part I. Since the secondary principles must be objective, there can be only one such valid set. This difficulty will be considered also.

Before coming round to the secondary principles, I shall explore what I take to be the central difficulty in the theory, with the aim of revealing an incoherence in it at a fundamental level. This incoherence springs from the way in which, as a consequence of the theory, the particular life of individuals is related to the moral life that binds them to others. It is an incoherence in relating the particular and general dimensions of men's lives. The particular choices of the individual (his particular will) and the content of his moral life (his moral will) are determined in quite separate and independent ways. The particular will[12] is to be determined by the individual in a relation to himself, unmediated by a relation to others and quite

---

[12] In talking in this way I do not presuppose the existence of some peculiar entity called the Will. By the will I mean the capacity of the individual to direct his behaviour in accordance with the conception of an end aimed at. The moral will is the exercise of this capacity in respect of the individual's recognition of the claims on him of other persons; the particular will is the exercise of this capacity in respect of his desires for his own life.

independently of the moral will, which, indeed, affirms the individual's common identity with others, their equal value, but does so quite abstractly. The latter is correspondingly determined independently of individuals' particular choices. This separate and independent identification of the particular and moral dimensions of individuals' lives involves the two dimensions in a radical opposition, and cannot sustain a coherent conception of the individual or of the individual's relations to others in community. It is the consequence of the view that the individual's particular life has value as the product of his own choice. Thus the value of his particular life consists in this relation to himself unmediated by a relation to others. At the same time the fact that he has value as the chooser of his own life requires the acknowledgement of the equal value of others. But this valuation of the lives of others is quite independent of the choice he makes for his own.

AUTHENTICITY

Since on the individualist theory individuals have value in respect of their capacity as self-formers, a particular life has moral worth only to the extent that the individual himself has chosen it. A man who merely grows into a particular way of life without reflecting on the ordering of values contained in it, and so without making himself responsible for it, has not chosen that life for himself, and hence that life has no moral worth. It is an inauthentic life, since it embodies the choices of others or 'society'.

Authenticity is a value intimately connected with the modern ethical idea. It does not arise where the source of moral value lies outside the individual in a principle to which the individual must conform his will. Authenticity expresses the idea that moral worth requires the individual to conform his will to himself, and not to something outside himself. In earlier, pre-Rousseauan forms of modern ethical theory the problem of authenticity does not arise because it is assumed in an uncritical way that the individual is free in doing what he wants. The question of how what he wants relates to the earlier choices of others and in particular to the form of society in which he has developed is not confronted. But this means only that the theorist unreflectively presupposes that the value of authenticity is immediately contained in whatever the individual wants. One form of this is the egoism to be found in Hobbes.

Authenticity requires that the individual in forming his particular life be for himself, and to the exclusion of all others, the only value by reference to which that life is chosen. This follows from the claim that the individual as such or in respect of his pure self-forming capacity is the source of value. If the individual chooses his life with a view to the realization in it of some value pertaining to an entity that is not himself, he necessarily subordinates his particular life to that other entity and makes his particular life a means to its self-realization. Whether this other entity is another individual, society, or indeed God, the subordination of oneself to it is the inauthentic renunciation of self-determination for determination by the other. This will be true even though one willingly renounces one's will in favour of the other. The fact that one chooses one's subordination does not make the choice an item in one's own self-determination, for to do that one would have to preserve the superiority of one's own value that is realized in the particular choice. This would mean that if one were to choose to subordinate oneself to God, then the service of God, and indeed God's value for one, would have to be seen as an item in the realization of a higher value, namely oneself. While this would be absurd in the case of God, it would be a way of accommodating the service of human others to the value of authenticity. So long as my benevolent acts towards others can be represented as choices I make for my life having regard only to myself as the value to be realized through those acts, they are compatible with the requirements of authenticity. Any choice whatsoever that can be meaningfully represented in this way will be so compatible.

It is at the level of particular life, in respect of the individual's particular choices, that the value of authenticity forbids one to have as the end of one's action, not oneself, but another. In respect of the moral or general dimension of the individual's life, the modern doctrine specifically requires the individual to treat others as ends for him. They are ends for him because they are ends *in themselves* or objective ends, and hence are ends for him in abstraction from or independently of any relation to his particular life. Thus the fact that at the particular level the individual is required not to have others as his end, while at the moral level he is so required, does not constitute an immediate and absurd contradiction. It reflects the fact that what one is required to do at the moral level is in the first instance to endorse whatever the other individual authentically chooses for himself, that is whatever he chooses having only himself as his end at the particular level. This disjunction between the two levels arises from the separation of them and will lead to their radical opposition and the deep-rooted incoherence of the theory.

EGOISM

In arguing that the authenticity requirement implicit in individualist ethics demands that the individual choose his life having regard only to himself as the value to be realized in it, it may look as though I am holding that the theory involves egoism at the particular level. There are, indeed, notable egoistic formulations of the individualist ethic in the early modern period, e.g. Hobbes, whom I will discuss later, but also classical economic theory.

Dumont, in an interesting book,[13] is concerned with the way in which the ethico-political ideas of freedom and equality are reflected in and are crucial to the development of an independent economic theory in its classic form. He argues that the direction classical economics took in e.g. Locke, Mandeville, Smith, as expressed in the labour theory of value, was towards conceiving of economic value as the product of the individual's relation to things or nature, and not as the product of his

[13] L. Dumont, *From Mandeville to Marx*, University of Chicago Press, 1977.

exchange relations with other men: the value of a thing is determined independently of the exchange relation. Clearly this view of the economic world is closely related to the developing ethical view of the world according to which the individual on his own is the creator of value in his particular life, and this value is not the product of his relation to other men. Since the individual is essentially oriented towards nature in his economic activity and not to other men, we must understand his exchange relations to others as means to the better satisfaction of his ends, defined in terms of his relation to nature. In this scheme, others cannot be ends of the individual's economic choices, and it is, then, natural enough to characterize the individual as purely self-interested.

In so far as the ends this self-interested individual is understood to pursue are constituted by his material needs, we are dealing with a fairly primitive and unsatisfactory version of his freedom. The more sophisticated version, which emphasizes that it is the individual's authentic choice of this or that, not what he chooses, that constitutes his independence of others, is not so obviously tied to the notion of self-interest. For, as I have argued above, the individual may choose to engage in benevolent activities in a way which satisfies the requirements of authenticity. But is it not the case that, even if one pursues non-selfish values, e.g. benevolent ones, in one's particular life, one has an overall attitude to one's particular life and to the values realized in it that can be called egoistic? Consider this issue in terms of a distinction made by Bernard Williams between I-desires and non-I desires.[14]

I-desires are desires for states of oneself which can always be expressed in the form: I desire that *I* have, possess or enjoy something, whereas non-I desires are desires for states of another being *X*, where what I desire is that *X* have, possess or enjoy something, and this desire cannot be reduced to a means to the attainment of some further I-desires. A benevolent life, then, involves, in the first instance, the having of non-I desires. But if

[14] B. Williams, 'Egoism and Altruism' in *Problems of the Self*, Cambridge University Press, 1973.

these benevolent non-I desires are to be understood as authentic expressions of the individual's personality, must they not be reducible in the end to I-desires? It is important to distinguish the reduction of what appears at first sight to be non-I desires to an I-desire at two different levels. Where I desire to bring about a good for B because I want B to do Y for me, and Y is a state of affairs in which I possess something, my desire to benefit B is merely a means to the satisfaction of an I-desire. In this case the reduction cancels the genuineness of the non-I desire, because the I-desire to which it is reduced is the same kind as the apparently non-I desire. It is a desire for some particular state of affairs.

Suppose, however, that my desire that B have X cannot be reduced to a means to my enjoying some further particular state Y. I want B to have X because this state of affairs is one of my choices for my life. In this way it enters as an element into a whole that I value, which is my self-formed life. What constitutes the value for me in realizing this choice of getting X for B is that it is a means of my realizing my free nature in a self-determined life. This is obviously not a case of simple or crude egoism, but is rather a sophisticated egoism on a much grander scale. In this sense individualist ethical theory requires egoism or the pursuit of private interest at the particular level.

THE PRINCIPLE OF EQUAL VALUE IN SOME CONTEMPORARY LITERATURE

The above account gives the main features of the form that the modern ethical idea takes in so far as it is expressed in individualist terms through the notions of freedom and equality. In the introduction I stated that a fundamental principle is an answer to the question: why should the individual limit himself by respect for the claims of others? The modern individualist answer to this question, then, is that the individual himself is the source of moral value expressed in the principle of the equal value of individuals. But since the point of view from which the question is raised is what I called the independent standpoint, from which the individual is an end only for himself, the answer must explain why the individual has any interest in limiting himself by respect for the source of moral value. The independent standpoint describes the free nature of the individual in its subjective form, and so this explanation involves showing why the individual has an interest in moving, or some reason to move, from the subjective form of freedom to the objective form: in other words it involves showing that he has reason to accept the principle of equality. The proof of equality is, thus, a necessity for the satisfactory grounding of individualist ethical thought, and I shall consider some recent articles to show how the issue arises and is unsatisfactorily explored, but also to bear out, in so far as a few more references to contemporary literature can, the above account of the main elements in individualist thought.

Before considering these articles, it is not irrelevant to show that the required proof of the equality principle could not possibly be met by any evidence as to the de facto equal or identical *particular* natures of men, that is to say by the doctrine held at one time, and seemingly still held by some people, in regard to the mind, that men are at conception identical genetic material on which different environmental experiences produce different effects and so differentiated men. Whether this is true or not, it cannot ground the moral equality of men, since in itself the fact contains no element of moral value at all. Suppose that it is true, then either the environment is not the same for everybody or it is. In the former case we are to suppose that the resulting inequalities between men are to be held unjust. Evidently some argument is needed to show how equal genetic endowment is to be translated into equal worth as an end of action. Otherwise there is no reason for men not to pursue and enjoy whatever differentiated advantage over others the environment offers them. But however hard and long we contemplate the fact of equal genetic endowment, no principle of equal value can be derived from it. If we had already established the principle of equal value, then the facts about genetic endowments can begin to feature in an argument about unequal environments. But they are not relevant to the determination of the fundamental principle. Indeed the logical and moral force of the idea of the equal value of men lies in its application to *all* men, however different they are in natural abilities, tastes and inclinations.

It is nevertheless true that men must have something in common, by virtue of which it is possible to argue that they have the same worth. What this something is should be clear: it is man's capacity for freedom. This freedom is part of man's empirical nature and has a subjective interpretation, but it is also that on which the objective interpretation of man's value is based. I now turn to some contemporary discussion of this problem.

Gewirth.[15] Gewirth intends to show how a principle of egalitarian justice can be established, which, in its minimal form, demands that 'all men irrespective of their different capacities or merits should have equal freedom to pursue their goals without violence to other men, equal possession of the necessities of life, equal opportunity to develop and utilize their talents to the fullest possible extent, equality of civil and political rights and so forth'.[16] This list combines the fundamental principle of equal value with both negative (non-interference with others' liberty) and positive (provision of opportunities to attain one's goals) interpretations of its requirements. But Gewirth's main concern is with the proof of a basic claim to an equal right to freedom, and I shall concentrate on this proof. His aim is to show that the equal right claim follows from certain rational requirements on actions.

Firstly he characterizes the notion of agency as it is the possible object of regulation by moral rules and judgements. Actions capable of being so regulated must be under the control of the agent, and hence must have two central features: (a)

---

[15] A. Gewirth, 'The Justification of Egalitarian Justice', *American Philosophical Quarterly*, vol. 8, No. 4, 1971. Gewirth has elaborated his argument in a book, but the essential position remains the same: *Reason and Morality*, University of Chicago Press, 1978.

[16] ibid., p. 331.

voluntariness, 'the agent who performs them must know what he is doing and must initiate or choose and control his behaviour without his choice being forced';[17] (b) purposiveness, 'the agent must intend to do what he does envisaging some purpose or goal'. The realization of the purpose the agent must see as some sort of good.

Secondly, it follows from this, according to Gewirth, that the agent regards his purpose as justifying his action to realize it, and claims implicitly that he has, at least, a prima facie right to perform the action. In the first part of this, the purpose of the agent is to be understood as constituting a reason for action, which for him necessarily justifies the action. Of course, this reason for action may be overruled by weightier reasons justifying some other action, but overruling does not obliterate the initial justifying relation between purpose and action. This part I shall take as uncontroversial. It is the second claim, which is supposed to follow directly from the first, that presents the problem. Gewirth holds, then, that it follows from the fact that the agent must see his action as justified by his purpose that he claims, implicitly, a right against others not to be interfered with in the performance of the action. 'For in so far as one regards one's purposes as good and hence as justifying one's action according to whatever criteria one accepts in the given context, one holds that according to those criteria, one's action should not be prevented from occurring by any other person.'[18]

The rest of Gewirth's argument is concerned to show that once the agent has made, or is committed implicitly to making, the right-claim against other agents not to be interfered with in the forming and pursuit of his purposes, he is obliged to acknowledge a like claim in others. The value of Gewirth's argument here lies in the way it spells out what the derivation of the equal right involves. The agent seeks to impose an obligation on other agents not to interfere, and the question is, on what basis can he do this? He must appeal to some characteristic either of his project or of himself. He might try to claim

[17] ibid., p. 332.
[18] ibid., p. 334.

his right on the grounds that his projects are of a particular nature, or that he is an agent of a particular kind, for example that he is a member of the Aryan race, or that his projects are aimed at realizing some substantive good. Since the agent is to be understood as making his claim to a right against all other agents, he must construct a rational principle that will rationally compel them to the course he requires. But any appeal to a principle which is based on a restricted conception of legitimate agency, that is on some particular quality of the agent's will, must to that extent, according to Gewirth, be arbitrary from a rational point of view. No reason that excludes either some projects or some agents from the principle of respect can be universally compelling. To hold that only the projects of Aryans are entitled to respect cannot be supported by reasons which no one could deny. It is this requirement for an adequate and rational justification which ensures that a restricted definition of the value of the agent's will must be arbitrary. Hence the only grounds, on which an individual could appeal to all other agents for respect, are those which identify him in his purely general character as an agent, the voluntary and purposive nature of his will. These are the essential features of agency, and it is only to these that the agent can appeal as a justification for his claim against all other agents as such. It follows directly from this rational requirement that the ground for the agent's claim to respect is equally a ground for all agents as such, and hence establishes, what Gewirth wanted to establish, the principle of a prima facie equal right of agents to pursue their projects without interference.

The error in Gewirth's reasoning consists in the claim that the agent's attitude to his action is to be understood, not subjectively as justifications *for him*, but objectively as justifications for anyone. If the objective interpretation of justification were necessary, it would be the case that the individual simply by virtue of his free rational agency was committed to claiming objective validity for his purposes, and hence would be forced by the power of reason to acknowledge an equal right in others. But Gewirth has absolutely no argument to show that the subjective interpretation of free agency makes no sense, and that we must consequently adopt the objective one. Indeed he begins by putting the justificatory nature of the purpose in subjective form, the purpose justifies the action *for him*, and immediately proceeds to interpret this justification in objective terms. Gewirth here is falling victim to the consequences of the modern moral view that grounds moral worth in the individual, that it has to treat the purposes of the individual as having objective worth by virtue of their being the purposes of an individual. Hence it seems impossible that one should be able to think of free agency as other than carrying with it the objective view.

Benn. Benn goes over similar issues in two recent articles. In the first[19] of these he aims at providing a justification for equality understood as the equal consideration of interests. He admits that men's equally valued interests will conflict, and that, therefore, further principles are required for ordering them in a just way. But his primary concern is with the justification of the initial principle that establishes the right of each to have his interests considered equally along with the interest of everybody else who is likely to be affected by a given action. This principle involves two parts: (a) that the agent considers other men's interests as *their* interests, and hence does not treat them simply as means to his own interests; (b) that the agent gives *equal* consideration to others' interests, since, Benn supposes, the agent could consider all men's interests, but unequally, in accordance with some elitist criterion. This last qualification seems to be unnecessary. For (a) should mean that the agent has to value the interests of others simply because they are the interests of individuals, who are ends in themselves. It would, then, follow that one must value them equally and not unequally in accordance with some elitist criterion, since to do the latter would not be to value interests simply as the interests of individuals.

---

[19] S. I. Benn, 'Egalitarianism and the Equal Consideration of Interests' in J. Roland Pennock and J. W. Chapman (eds.), *Equality: Nomos IX*, Atherton Press, 1967.

Benn's point is clear enough, however: equality means equal consideration of the interests of men in virtue of their being men or in virtue of their pure humanity. This is fundamental, Benn says, to the idea of social equality, which is to be understood as an equality of esteem, and which he expresses in this way: 'I am as good as anybody else; I may not be as clever or hardworking as you are, but I am as good as you are.'[20] This equality of esteem does not mean that we are respecting people for possessing some distinguished quality, which in fact all men have. It means that every man is entitled to be taken on his own merits, that is to say as he values himself. Here we have the modern idea, that I have been concerned to elicit, expressed in undisguised crudity.

How is this idea of equal worth to be established? In answer to this, Benn presents a picture of man as a rational being, who, by making responsible choices among possible ways of life, is capable of moral freedom and so makes himself into a being worthy of respect. The capacity to choose one's own way of life is the characteristic human enterprise and requires an ability to appraise and criticize oneself. Here, then, is another example of the view that the individual person brings moral value into being through his capacity for freedom.

The problem remains as to why the individual's empirical capacity for freedom should *ipso facto* be the source of moral worth. Benn, like Gewirth, simply does not see the problem. For what he says is that the individual sees in others the image of himself, and so sees that other men have interests and capacities which give them claims of precisely the same kind as he makes on his own behalf. This last point is the crucial one. Yet Benn does not tell us what the claims one makes on one's own behalf are, and why one must make them. Obviously he has in mind that the individual claims for his responsible choices of a way of life that others respect his choice because it is the choice of an individual choosing his own way of life and so on. Given such a claim, it follows that, if other men are the images of oneself and have the same nature, one must grant

[20] ibid., p. 69. He is quoting J. C. Davies with approval.

31

them what one claims for oneself. But why must the individual make this claim for himself?

In a later article[21] Benn addresses himself to this question and comes round to the view that the claim to respect, on which the justification of equality is based, is not inherent in the notion of agency itself. He begins with an account of the characteristics of man as chooser or decision-maker, the details of which we need not consider, since for the purposes of my consideration of this argument they do not alter anything already said above about the notion of agency. The relevant characteristic of man is his ability to formulate and pursue projects for his life. Benn aims to justify two principles, the first of which he calls the principle of respect for autarchy, by which he means respect for men in virtue of their capacity as formers and pursuers of projects for their lives. He describes what he calls a natural person: a natural person is a free, purposive agent, aware of himself as an initiator of events. Respect for autarchy is respect for men as natural persons. This is the primary moral principle that requires justification before we proceed to its further development as the principle of autonomy, which he understands as an ideal of personality, involving freedom in a fuller sense than can be attributed to the natural person.

For my immediate purposes it is the argument for the primary moral principle of equal respect for natural persons, that is the interesting one. Unless this can be established, autonomy is irrelevant. We are back with the problem of why the free agent, or here the natural person, should claim respect from others, and hence be committed to acknowledge equal worth in others. But now Benn accepts that a natural person could see other persons as beings like himself, having enterprises that are as important to them as his own are for himself, and yet that 'this would still not be enough to commit him to an appreciation of their enterprises as reasons for action or forbearance for him too'.[22] This might be, he says, a Hobbesian state of nature

[21] S. I. Benn, 'Freedom, Autonomy and the Concept of a Person', *Proceedings of the Aristotelian Society*, 1975–6.
[22] ibid., p. 119.

in which no one made or acknowledged right-claims in his relations with others.[23]

In this way Benn accepts the subjective formulation of free agency and rejects Gewirth's and his own previous sliding from the subjective to the objective formulation under the guise of the requirements of reason. If reason does not require this move, what does? Benn sees that the first step in an adequate account involves the individual in claiming respect as a natural person: 'claiming respect, moral personality, on the grounds of natural personality,[24] we are then, committed to extending it to anyone else satisfying the same conditions'.[25] Why, then, should the individual claim respect? Benn's answer is that a person not claiming and according respect would be unable to experience the reactive feelings and attitudes of interpersonal relations: there would be no love or friendship, no capacity for resentment or indignation at one's treatment by others, and so on.

This argument appeals to the rich emotional life that a person would be missing if he did not enter into moral relations with others. This seems to treat the emotions referred to as not themselves moral, and the recognition of moral value as the means whereby this apparently higher value is to be realized. If this were the case, then the argument would involve the absurdity of attempting to justify moral value, which is acknowledged to be the ground of the value in interpersonal relations, in terms of lesser values that it grounds. But perhaps the highly valued emotional life is to be understood as the central element within the moral life, on account of which it is to be valued. In that case we would have no argument at all justifying the adoption of the moral standpoint. For, in effect, Benn would be saying that if we do not adopt the moral standpoint, we will be missing the moral life!

Williams. Williams's article[26] on equality has received attention

23 The natural person is in effect the individual from the independent standpoint.

24 i.e. one's natural choices are of moral worth.   25 ibid., p. 121.

26 B. Williams, 'The Idea of Equality' in P. Laslett and W. Runciman (eds.), *Politics, Philosophy and Society II*, Basil Blackwell, 1962.

and respect, but much of the article is concerned with the interpretation of the requirements of equality, once the principle has been accepted, in particular with the idea of equality of opportunity, which I shall not discuss here. He begins by rejecting Kant's detachment of the moral worth of agents from all contingent characteristics of them, and his commitment to a transcendental view of their worth. His reason is that it seems empty to say that all men are equal as moral agents when questions relevant to their moral capacities, for instance, their responsibility for their actions, have an empirical reference. If men have in fact unequal capacities in this respect, how can they be equal as moral agents?

He proposes to justify not the concept of equal worth as moral agents, but that of equal respect as men, where nothing is to be included in the notion of man which is not an empirical characteristic. His major point to this end is that individuals have points of view on the world consisting in their own conception of their lives. Respect for men is valuing them, not in terms of their technical excellence as engineers, sportsmen or whatever, for which men are in fact and unavoidably valued unequally, but from their own point of view of themselves.

Williams says that these are vague notions, but he believes that they mark out the direction of a justification of equality. This is to be done by bringing the point to bear on the relation between a man's self-understanding and the conception of him formed by his society. In so far as an individual's self-conception is not his own but his society's imposed on him, respect is not being paid to the individual. A peasant in a pre-modern hierarchical society develops a view of himself as essentially a being of this type, having a definite subordinate identity and role in his social whole. This self-understanding of the peasant is produced in him by his society. It is not one that he has produced for himself. The peasant, unaware of his society, may be happy enough, but were he to become aware of this fact he would no longer be able to identify with his society's view of him. Williams wants to conclude from this that if an individual is to see himself correctly, as responsible for his own self-conception, he must conceive himself as essentially equal in his fundamental relations to others. Hence a society founded on equality, rather than on hierarchy, can alone be justified.

This argument clearly presupposes that the individual is in himself something different from being a peasant, lord, capitalist etc., but what this nature is Williams only points to through his notion of the individual's own point of view on the world. It seems obvious enough, however, that this essential character, in virtue of which respect is due a man, must consist in the individual's having no *determinate* character, but in his capacity to give a character to himself. Since respect involves seeing him from his own point of view, this must mean valuing him in terms of the purposes he gives himself for his life. If he chooses for himself the life of a peasant farmer, then this would be his authentic choice for his life.

Thus we see that the only reasonable development of Williams's notion of the individual's point of view on the world takes us back to the central ideas of individualist ethics consisting in the individual giving his value to himself.[27] On Williams's view it must be the case that because an individual has the empirical capacity to conceive and pursue a life of his own, he is deserving of moral respect. But this, as should now be obvious, begs the question as to why the empirical capacity for freedom by itself involves a claim to respect.

In a later article, already referred to,[28] Williams does directly confront the question begged in the first article. He does so in the form, not of a justification of equality, but of a justification of the moral standpoint or what he calls altruism. By altruism he means the treatment of the interests of others as such as making some claim on one. The question of how altruism is to be justified is thus equivalent to the question that I pose from

---

[27] There are innumerable books and articles in the contemporary literature in which this position is to be found in some form. For a sample see: R. H. Tawney, *Equality*, Unwin Books, 1964; J. Rees, *Equality*, Macmillan, 1972; J. Wilson, *Equality*, Hutchinson, 1966; G. Vlastos, 'Justice and Equality' in R. Brandt (ed.), *Social Justice*, Prentice-Hall, 1962, as also in the works already referred to by Rawls, Nozick, Dworkin and Lukes.

[28] 'Egoism and Altruism'. See p. 24 above.

the independent standpoint, and in so far as altruism is understood to be a principle affirming that the interests of men as such have a claim to respect, it is equivalent to the principle of equality. As Williams presents the issue, it concerns the question of how it is possible to show to a man who begins by denying that others as such have any claims on him at all that he should recognize such claims. This initial position Williams calls egoism. He rejects the rationalist answer to this question.

Williams takes the rationalist argument up in this form: the egoist, who holds that the interests of a man constitute reasons for action for him but not for anyone, is forced into an inconsistency when his interests conflict with those of another. He is forced to admit that others have reason to act in a way detrimental to himself. But, as Williams argues, the egoist is not committed, by the acceptance that a man's interests are reasons for him to act and hence that another has a reason to act contrary to his own interest in case of conflict, to the view that it is *right* for the other to act contrary to his interests, where right has objective force, being a reason for anyone, but only that the other has *subjectively* a reason so to act. The egoist's attitude to the other, as Williams correctly characterizes it, is that the other can, if he wishes, try to act contrary to his interests; the egoist is not going to complain if he does. But the egoist is certainly not going to stand back and allow the other to do so. In so far as there is any right here, it is the subjective Hobbesian right of nature to take any measure for one's own preservation (in pursuit of one's interests) which involves no obligation on others to limit their interest by respect for it.

This brings out the rationalist argument's dependence on conflating the subjective and objective version of a reason for action, that we have already seen in the case of Gewirth and implicit in the first Benn article. Williams has his own idea as to how the move towards altruism can be made. This is through the distinction between I-desires and non-I desires that I have already referred to.[29] Williams affirms that it is a fact about human beings that they have non-I desires for the welfare of

[29] See p. 24 above.

others. If so, we can see that they are already disposed to pursue the good of others, and it would not be as big a step from here to a generalized altruism, as it is from pure egoism involving nothing but I-desires to the having of non-I desires. With non-I desires men are already on the road to altruism.

The difficulty with this argument is, in the first place, that we are not given an account of the transition that needs to be made from non-I desires for particular persons to a generalized altruism, and hence we are unclear as to the moral status of non-I desires. For they could already contain within them the moral attitude to the other, and their only defect from the moral point of view would be the lack of generalization in this attitude. This would be the case, if in pursuing the welfare of this or that particular person we have feelings of disinterested love towards that person through which we treat his good as in itself a reason for us to act.

Thus our attitude towards his good is the moral one that it is as such a reason for us to act, but because the attitude in this case is based on a feeling for a *particular* person it obviously cannot be made to include all men as such. The way in which this account would have to be developed, then, would be through a notion of a generalized feeling for others, and that would make it a version of the sympathy theory of ethics which I shall consider shortly.[30]

But we could understand particular non-I desires in the manner discussed above,[31] according to which non-I desires are elements in an individual's authentic choice of a life. They would then be elements in an egoism on a grander scale, and the problem of the move from egoism to altruism would in no way be reduced by the supposition that such non-I desires exist.

[30] See below pp. 51–5.
[31] See pp. 21–5 above.

THE MOTIVATIONAL
STRUCTURE OF MORALITY

In his book *The Possibility of Altruism*[32] Nagel seeks an explanation of the basic principles of ethics which will account for the motivational force of ethics. These basic principles he calls altruism, used in the sense Williams gives it in his article. Nagel insists that what is required is an explanation and not a justification for the basic principles. His reason is that the demand for a justification suggests that one must provide an account of why the moral principles *should* be obligatory on individuals, and this involves the absurd requirement of finding a moral justification for morality. An explanation, on the other hand, will provide an account of how ethical considerations can have motivational force, that is to say what it is about them that produces appropriate action in men. This would not be a moral justification, but a demonstration of how, starting with a motivational structure for man which represents him as a non-moral but free rational agent, moral considerations tie into that structure. The demonstration of the possibility of morality involves showing how the subjective understanding of the self-valuing individual is connected with and subordinated to the objective understanding.

Nagel distinguishes two types of approach to this question: an internalist and an externalist.[33] The internalist holds that the presence of a motivation for acting morally is guaranteed by the truth of ethical propositions themselves. This assumes that it has been shown how ethical considerations connect up with the non-moral motivational structure of men. Given that they do in one way or another, a true ethical proposition will itself be a reason for action. The externalist, on the other hand, denies that ethical considerations of themselves motivate: some additional psychological sanction is necessary. On the externalist view one can acknowledge a moral obligation and at the same

---

[32] T. Nagel, *The Possibility of Altruism*, Clarendon Press, 1970.
[33] ibid., p. 7.

time ask whether one has any reason for fulfilling it. Thus there cannot be a moral motive for moral action, and, consequently, if the possibility of morality is to be understood in terms of the possibility of acting from a moral motive, the externalist view in effect denies that morality is possible.

I shall follow Nagel in considering only internalist views. One such view, that Nagel refers to, however, I shall not consider. This is the view that rejects moral objectivity, and builds motivational content into the meaning rather than the truth of ethical assertions. Ethical assertions, on this view, are expressions of a special sort of inclination. Since such a theory of ethics is essentially anti-rational, it is incapable of providing an explanation of the peculiar validity of an individualist ethics in which the equality principle must be founded on more than an arbitrary choice. The internalist views that I shall consider are those that reveal most clearly the structure of individual thought and the difficulties in it. A subjectivist of the above kind may try to uphold individualist values of freedom and equality as expressions of a basic inclination of individuals, but he cannot explain why we must attach ourselves to these values rather than any other. At the most he can only reject non-individualist values as those of a fanatic. But this is hardly a weighty argument.

Attempts to explain why individualist values are necessary are the object of my interest, and I shall consider the three main internalist strategies of an objectivist nature that Nagel distinguishes: self-interest, sympathy and rationalism. Furthermore, I shall consider these strategies in the form they take in the ethical doctrines of Hobbes, Rousseau and Kant respectively. There is a logical development in the individualist arguments that these writers present, because each is responding to the perceived unsatisfactoriness of the earlier view. In this development we can see the radical incoherence in individualist thought.

I shall, of course, be treating these past writers as philosophers of contemporary relevance. There are those who consider that to treat a past writer philosophically is, in effect, not to say anything about the historical figure whose views one purports to be criticizing, but only about an intellectual construction from one's present standpoint.[34] Presumably this rejection of the meaningfulness of a philosophical treatment of a past writer is based upon the absence of a shared historical context between past writer and present commentator. It is obviously not inappropriate to engage philosophically with a writer of the immediate past, even though from some standpoint the historical context would not be the same for past and present writer. Thus, if the concerns of the present writer were the same as those of the philosophical writers of the seventeenth and eighteenth centuries being discussed, there would be a shared historical context, and the Pocockian criticism would become irrelevant: Hobbes, Rousseau and Kant would be our contemporaries. It is the argument of this work that the fundamental concerns of Hobbes and others are identical with the unresolved, if not explicit, problems of our contemporary philosophical world. If this is not immediately obvious, it is because the twentieth century may be said by and large to have given up hope, or to deny the possibility, of finding a satisfactory grounding for the individualist values that it is nevertheless content to affirm in a subjective and irrationalist manner.[35]

In discussing the three internalist strategies of self-interest, sympathy and rationalism in and through the work of Hobbes, Rousseau and Kant, my aim is to bring out the development that occurred in attempts to relate self-interest and morality. One answer to the problem of the motivational force of morality consists in attempting to show that the structure of moral reason forms a part of a more sophisticated structure of self-interested reason. The rejection of this view leads in the thought first of Rousseau and then of Kant to the recognition that if morality is to be possible its motivational force must be independent of self-

---

[34] J. G. A. Pocock, *Politics Language, and Time*, Methuen, 1971, pp. 5–9. See also Q. Skinner, 'Meaning and Understanding in the History of Ideas', *History and Theory*, 1969, and also J. Dunn, 'The Identity of the History of Ideas', *Philosophy*, 1968. For some sensible remarks on this issue see B. Williams's preface to his *Descartes*, Penguin Books, 1978.

[35] There are, of course, tentative efforts in this direction, some of which I have already considered.

interest and must be tied to the development of another element in the human personality; and this itself leads to a radical opposition between the structures of moral and of self-interested reason, and so between the elements of the self.

HOBBESIAN EGOISM

One can elicit from Hobbes's work an argument with a fairly clear structure designed to show that the constraints of morality, in the form of organized civil society based on natural laws requiring respect for the rights of others, are part of self-interested rationality. The motivational force of morality is, then, explicable in terms of the unquestioned motivational force of self-interest. It is, of course, possible to interpret Hobbes's egoism in the light of the discussion above on the distinction between I-desires and non-I desires, which incorporates benevolent acts within an overall egoism. As regards interpretations of Hobbes which deny his egoism, reasons for such interpretations will be mentioned later and be met at that point.

Men, according to Hobbes, are self-maintaining systems driven into constant activity by the impact on them of new objects of desire and aversion in sense-experience. Their aim is not simply the attainment of the immediate object of desire, but rather self-preservation, in which the object is the assurance of the way of future desire. Since power over both nature and men is a man's present means to obtain some future good, and since men find themselves in conflict in their drive for self-preservation, there is in man a 'restless desire of power after power, that ceaseth only in death'.[36] This opposition of men's powers in the 'natural condition of mankind' leads to a constant and unremitting war of every man against every man. The de facto equality of their powers, in the sense that no one is strong enough not to be at the mercy of any other, ensures that this competition cannot be resolved through natural domination.[37] The state of war is the product of the inherent tendency of

[36] T. Hobbes, *Leviathan*, Basil Blackwell, 1955, p. 64.
[37] ibid., pp. 80–1.

men's natures, which underlies all social life, and which would break out in unrestrained form were it not held in check by the devices of a commonwealth. A commonwealth, because it opposes this tendency in human nature that leads to destruction and death, is to be derived from the nature of man in multitudes, since it constitutes the rationally necessary conditions for men to preserve themselves in multitudes. The general form of the argument for including morality in self-interest is, thus, that each man by nature seeks to preserve himself; whatever is a necessary condition of self-preservation serves the individual's self-interest; a commonwealth, and in other words ethical and political life, are necessary conditions of self-preservation, and hence are in each man's self-interest.

The more detailed reasoning to this end includes two types of argument; one concerned with natural laws, and the other with institutional arrangements including sovereign authority for elaborating these natural laws in an enforced and effective system of legislation. The argument for natural laws has logical priority, since without a foundation in them the position of the Sovereign has no validity. A law of nature, Hobbes says, is a 'precept or general rule, found out by reason, by which a man is forbidden to do that, which is destructive of his life'.[38] Whether this obligation is prudential or moral is, of course, the question to be considered. The difficulty of deciding it arises from the fact that the natural laws appear both to form part of an overall structure of prudential reasoning and to constitute an account of the basic structure of morality. Thus Hobbes specifically calls them eternal laws of good and evil, virtue and vice, and the science of them the science of moral philosophy.[39]

In determining the kind of rationality that is supposed to be exhibited in Hobbes's laws of nature, one must distinguish three elements in their structure: (1) the reasoning which leads up to men's conception of the laws of nature as possible or necessary rules to follow in their mutual relations; (2) the nature and

---

[38] ibid., p. 84.
[39] ibid., p. 104. They can also be seen as the commands of God, but this seems to be optional.

content of the rules; (3) the motive men have for following the rules. Thus under (1) it is clear that the rules of natural law are to be understood as arrived at through a process of prudential reasoning by the individual about the consequences of his natural condition. That is to say were men to reason correctly about the conditions necessary for their self-preservation, they would conclude that the rules of natural law are necessary conditions. Thus men conceive, and may be said to propose to each other, a life in accordance with natural law, in the form of prudential reasoning. But this fact alone determines neither that the content of natural law will have the nature of self-interest, nor that the motive men have for actually abiding by the law will be a self-interested one.

By the content of natural law I mean, not the specific rules commanded, but the fact that an obligation is incurred through one's submission to natural law. Consider the three-fold distinction above in terms of the making and keeping of a promise. We may suppose that the promisor initially conceives of making the promise in self-interested terms: he hopes to gain something from the promise. But having made the promise, he incurs an obligation to keep the promise. The nature of the obligation, or in other words how we are to interpret the fact of the promisor's obligation, is not immediately clear, but that there is an obligation is not in dispute. At least, Hobbesian egoism as an account of how morality is possible does not question the existence of obligations. It is an *explanation* of those obligations. It explains how they have motivational force by showing how they are related to the unquestioned motivational force of self-interest. If there is an obligation, which may be open to explanation in terms of self-interest, it is not immediately obvious that this explanation is the correct one, simply because the initial motive for conceiving the promise was a self-interested motive.

Let us leave this side of the issue for the moment, and consider what Hobbes's rules of Natural Law require of us. They involve certain basic commitments which would be common ground to any individualist theory, whether egoistic or not. The 2nd Law of Nature is the most important one in this respect. It affirms that each man must be 'contented with so much liberty against other men, as he would allow other men against himself'.[40] It is a version of the idea of equal liberty, which I have been claiming is fundamental to the modern individualist moral conception. It establishes that in so far as one demands of others that they do not interfere in one's pursuit of self-preservation, one must acknowledge in them an equal right with oneself.

It might be thought that, since the equal right in this theory is 'created' by men, Hobbes is adopting a relativist position in which the value of each individual is not self-determined but mutually determined by an agreement. Of course, we are not to understand this as meaning that an actual agreement between men could be the foundation of men's equal right. The 'agreement' to an equal right represents the rationally necessary conditions for each to preserve himself in a competitive environment. It is implicit in such an environment, and only necessary for individuals to recognize and act upon. One side of these conditions is that one claims for oneself a freedom to pursue one's interests without impediment by others; the other side is that such a freedom is possible only if a like freedom is granted to all. The issue here is similar to that raised in the discussions above of the derivation of a principle of equal right in the articles of Gewirth, Benn and Williams, especially in Benn's second article. The initial stance with which 'natural persons' face each other is a purely subjective one, in which no rights against others are claimed. Benn's problem was why natural persons should begin to claim rights for themselves. Once they do this, the conclusion that an equal right is the basis of co-operative social relations cannot be avoided. In Hobbes's case also an initial subjectivity of stance is to be overcome by the mutual acknowledgement of an equal right (together with further conditions, of course) and this involves a basic claim by each for himself not to be interfered with together with an acceptance of the equal right of others. Thus the Law of Nature requires each man to claim for himself *a right residing in*

[40] ibid., p. 85.

himself as an independent individual in the world seeking his self-preservation, and to acknowledge a like right in others. Therein lies Hobbes's individualism naturally expressed in the principle of equal liberty. The right that each has is dependent on the moment of recognition, or in other words on the covenant to restrict one's unlimited right of nature, but what is thus recognized is a right residing in the individual as such. In this principle of equal right there is contained the principle of altruism in its negative form, the principle that an equal value attaches to the interests of others as to one's own, and hence that one cannot claim a greater liberty than others.[41] Thus the 2nd Law of Nature makes it clear that in so far as Hobbes's theory is an egoistic one, it is an egoistic theory of how what is widely accepted as a basic form of morality is possible. It is not a theory which holds that moral considerations are irrelevant.

The 3rd Law of Nature requires men to perform their covenants made. The 2nd, as we have seen, requires men to enter into an agreement to lay down their right to all things and accept a mutual limitation on the basis of the equal liberty principle. Once this agreement has been made, the 3rd Law imposes an obligation on those making it to keep it. This Hobbes roundly affirms. Without this obligation 'covenants are in vain and but empty words'.[42] Of course, we are still uncertain as to how to interpret the obligation, but that there is an obligation created by a covenant Hobbes leaves us in no doubt.[43] If we assume, as I have argued above, that the nature and content of obligatory agreements is at least not necessarily the same as the motive for entering them, we may begin to think that Hobbes has a doctrine, admittedly not very well developed,

---

41 While Hobbes's formulation of the 2nd Law of Nature stresses only that whatever liberty there is must be equal, and thus allows for the mutual acceptance of hardly any liberty, the only reasonable interpretation is that each would seek to maximize equal liberty, since there would be no advantage in restricting equal liberty when this does not contribute to self-preservation.   42 ibid., p. 93.

43 The obligation is in the first instance and until the sovereign comes into operation only in foro interno, not in foro externo. See for an extended discussion of this H. Warrender, *The Political Philosophy of Hobbes*, Clarendon Press, 1957.

of the nature of moral concepts, that has nothing to do with the egoistic psychology with which it is found connected in the text. We may arrive at the view that for Hobbes the moral concepts can be defined without reference to prudential considerations, and that they constitute a structure of rationality quite independent of self-interest.[44]

This is a most implausible view of what Hobbes is attempting to do. The mistake in it arises from the fact noted above that Hobbes's egoistic theory is nevertheless a theory of what are recognizably moral practices, and not a denial that morality is possible. Since we normally think of moral reason as distinct from and always potentially opposed to self-interest, we may conclude from Hobbes's undoubted use of ordinary moral language that he has a moral theory that is independent of his egoistic psychological theory.

It is, of course, the case that what Hobbes is attempting to do looks paradoxical, that is to incorporate the structure of moral reasoning within that of egoistic reasoning, and hence subordinate what is generally taken to be the higher element to what it is supposed to discipline. But if we accept that this is precisely what he aims to do, then we can see that he will need to preserve the formal obligatory nature of moral reasoning, e.g. that covenants made oblige of themselves, and at the same time that he will need to explain why covenants oblige within the terms of a general theory of self-interest.

Thus it seems to me that Hobbes wishes to combine in his theory both the idea of relations between persons generally called moral, involving reciprocal obligations arising from the very existence of these relations, and the idea that the motive for entering into these moral relations, and for keeping the commitments involved, is self-interest. This combination is incoherent. The problem produced by the attempted combination can be posed in this way.[45] Can obligation ever be contrary to

---

[44] See A. E. Taylor, 'The Ethical Doctrine of Hobbes' in K. C. Brown (ed.), *Hobbes Studies*, Basil Blackwell, 1965.

[45] I follow quite closely here D. Gauthier, *The Logic of Leviathan*, Clarendon Press, pp. 94–8.

prudence? If the answer to this is yes, then while Hobbes would have an account of a genuine moral obligation that account would make obligation and self-interest part company, and his system as an attempted unification of the two would break down. That system requires an obligation, which is both genuinely moral and is always in accordance with self-interest. We cannot, of course, say that one has an obligation only when it accords with one's self-interest, for this cancels the obligatory nature of the moral practices, e.g. keeping covenants, and so instead of explaining how moral practices are possible, renders them null.

The answer to the question posed above, if the aim of the theory is to be fulfilled, must be that obligation can never as a matter of fact be contrary to self-interest. The trouble with this is not so much its implausibility as the fact that it is possible to show that it could never be in the individual's self-interest to fulfil the obligations arising from his entry into moral practices. This is the argument from the theory of games.[46] The argument claims that, while egoists can see that they would be better off making an agreement to restrict their mutual invasions, nevertheless it would not be in their interest individually to keep the agreement. The issue is not whether it is in the interest of the individual to make the agreement, but whether it is in his interest to keep it. Assuming that the agreement is made, each individual will be better off if *all* keep the agreement. However, each will be even better off if all the others keep the agreement and he does not, since he will have the advantage of not being bound to perform something for them. It follows, then, that it cannot be in any individual's interest to keep the agreement. This will be true, whatever the others do. For, if they keep the agreement, then the individual will be better off not keeping it. If they do not, it would be absurd for him to do so. Since the position is the same for each individual, the agreement could not be made effective.

Hobbes certainly sees this difficulty, and aims to provide for

[46] See for a full and technical account in relation to Hobbes D. Gauthier, op. cit., pp. 77–89.

it through the device of a discipline external to the individual, which, by punishing breaches of the agreement, will give men a new motive for keeping it that will be stronger than their interest in not keeping it. This discipline is the power, created by a covenant of every man with every man, whereby each renounces his right to all things in favour of a man or body of men, who thereby becomes sovereign. The covenant creating the sovereign authorizes him to act on his creators' behalf, and they incur an obligation to each other to maintain this authorization. Each is obliged to his fellow covenanters to create and maintain the Sovereign power by which he is coerced into pursuing what is in any case his own interest. He is obliged to support the power which forces him to be free.

But the identical problem arises in relation to this obligation. For the power by which the Sovereign coerces his creators into keeping the agreements of Natural Law (not to invade each other) does not spring into existence immediately on the making of the covenant by which he is given authority to act. It arises only through individuals supporting, or not hindering, the Sovereign in his attempts to exercise power to enforce the Natural Law. In so far as this involves (a) helping the Sovereign to enforce the Law against others, and (b) allowing the Sovereign to enforce it against oneself, the self-interest of the individual would ensure that the Sovereign could never gain the support necessary to make his function effective. For (a) would involve risk and loss to oneself, and hence if others support the Sovereign, it will not be in one's interest to do so; while if others do not, it would be absurd for one to do so. On the other hand (b) is self-evidently contrary to one's interest.

This argument is paradoxical. For, although it is in each man's interest to live in a commonwealth, and so to make those covenants through which it can come into being, the argument shows that it is nevertheless contrary to each man's interest to keep the agreement. The paradoxical nature of this conclusion is often too easily dismissed on the grounds that it follows from the independent action of each individual; whereas what is required is some force which will overcome this independence by tying men's actions together.[47] It is certainly true that this is what is required to make the moral practice possible that is the foundation of men's association. But it hardly removes the paradox of game theory that each man can correctly reason that he would be better off in situation X, and can see what it is necessary to do to bring about situation X, and yet as conditions Y preparatory to the production of situation X come into being he can now correctly reason that his interest lies in acting in such a way as to frustrate the production of situation X. There must be an incoherence in the reasoning which yields such a result.

The incoherence can be explained in this way: we are to suppose that the men who conceive and make the agreement to limit natural right are egoists, purely self-concerned, who, dissatisfied with their natural condition, conceive of the rules of Natural Law as an improvement. At no point in thinking up and making the agreement is their egoistic attitude to each other abandoned or altered. This is the basic error which produces the incoherence. For, in conceiving of the agreement, they must conceive of something which alters their relation to each other, something which of itself binds them together. Otherwise, they have thought of nothing at all, empty words, as Hobbes says. But their conception of being bound by the agreement involves the idea of the other parties to the agreement having claims on one, and so of one's having to act by reference to their claims. And this means in effect that one has abandoned in idea the egoistic attitude towards others, and conceived of one's relations to them being founded on another attitude – that of equality. One has conceived of a situation in which one's private interest is to be pursued within the limits of a set of rules which tie one to others. Hence one's purely private interest is limited by and subject to the bond which unites one with others. To make and keep this agreement is to give reality to one's thought of a non-egoistic relation to others. How this reality is possible is no doubt still obscure, but one does not have to accept

---

[47] See J. L. MacKie, *Ethics*, Penguin Books, 1977, pp. 115–16; and also D. Gauthier, op. cit., p. 87.

the absurdity of supposing that the idea of such a relation can be thought by men who are pure egoists and who as such have no conception of the claims of others, and so worry about men who make an agreement to create such a relation, but who cannot keep the agreement.

The idea of a new rule-governed relation between men involves that of a new interest which is not purely the individual's, but is common to him and others, not in the sense of the coincidence of several independent self-interests, but in the sense of a unity or singleness of interest in which self and others are comprehended. Since this unity must be the basis on which each individual subsequently pursues his private interest, it must take priority over private interest, and subordinate private interest to itself. These are the conditions of men's abandoning egoism for altruism and cannot be represented as a more elaborate form of egoism. They require a radical alteration of the self, and a reorientation of thought away from the individual self and its interest to the common interest.

One may say that Hobbes's theory contains such a notion of the common interest and of the altered person necessary for its realization in the conception of the Sovereign Will, which includes all citizens within it, and to which citizens are bound and subordinated. The Sovereign's Will is, of course, the citizen's own creation, so that the citizen, in being subject to the Sovereign, is subject only to his own will.[48] But one cannot conclude from this that the Sovereign Will is simply the expression of the individual's egoistic interest, as Hobbes wishes us to do. For it is the individual's interest only in so far as it is the joint interest of the several creators of the sovereign: it is the individual's interest as this co-creator. It is not his interest as an individual who is quite separate from and independent of others, but only as he binds himself to others and thereby creates with others a new identity and interest for himself. This provides us with a distinction between the individual's interest as a particular individual within the whole, and his interest, shared with others, as co-creator of the whole. This

[48] Hobbes, op. cit., pp. 112 and 116.

distinction is necessary to make intelligible the subordination of the individual to the whole. Hobbes has, as I have indicated, the elements of this distinction, but cannot carry it through, since his aim is always to reduce the new self as co-creator of the whole to the old independent ego.

This systematic attempt to explain the requirements of community in terms of self-interest is of great value. What lies behind and informs Hobbes' persistence in this enterprise is the felt necessity to integrate the common interest of the individual as member of the whole with his particular interest as private person. It is not a satisfactory solution to the problem of how morality is possible, to acknowledge the coming into being of a new common self and interest, if this new self then parts company with the old private self and sets up an opposition and incoherence within the individual personality, which will be present also in the community. There must be some way of harmonizing the two selves. Hobbes strove to conceive this necessary harmony in terms of the new as a further expression of the old.

BENEVOLENCE AND SYMPATHY

One reaction to Hobbes's attempt to ground altruism in self-interest was (and no doubt still is) to attribute to man, besides the inclination to self-interest, a quite distinct sentiment of benevolence. Self-interest and benevolence are natural impulses in the human constitution. This removes the difficulty. The answer to the question, how morality is possible, is simple — men have a natural impulse to morality!

That man is capable of moral action, by which I mean capable of acting for the good of others, is certain; the philosophical question is not whether or not the capacity exists; but how we are to explain it: what is it in man that makes it possible? This question is one about the relation of morality, and its springs of action, to self-love. To say that we understand morality as the product of a special impulse to morality, does not tell us anything about how that impulse and its superstructure of moral rationality is related to the equivalent forms of self-love. On the contrary, it produces a view of man as governed by two quite separate and opposed impulses.

Why is it necessary, in order to explain morality philosophically, to show how it is related to self-interested rationality? To ask this is only to raise the question of the independent standpoint again as the starting point for philosophical reflection on ethics. If this is the starting point, then a demonstration of the possibility of morality must show how morality can be integrated with the demands of self-love. Hobbes's system would be ridiculous were not this the requirement. In effect the requirement is to show how the self can be related to the other in such a way that the self can pursue the interest of the other as though it were its own interest; in other words, to show how a common interest, a unity of self and other, is possible. This Hobbes attempts to do by integrating the other into the self, and making the other into an extension of the self, although this enlarged personality turns out to be the mighty Leviathan which includes them all.

Given this requirement the positing of a special impulse of benevolence is trite. The notion of sympathy as an explanation of the possibility of morality, however, is an advance on benevolence, in so far as it purports to provide an account of how self-love is transposed into the love of the other. Sympathy relates the love of others to self-love by positing a mechanism through which we are led to perceive others as beings like ourselves, suffering pain and feeling pleasure, as a result of which we are disturbed by their pain and pleased by their pleasures. For Hume the mechanism is the association of ideas by which the perception of the pain of the other gets translated into an equivalent pain in ourselves, and hence into a tendency to act to remove the cause of the pain in ourselves, which is the pain in the other.[49] We feel the pain or pleasure of others as though it were our own, and in so far as we act for their welfare, we can be said to be loving ourselves in them. In this way the unity of self and others that morality requires is created.

[49] Hume, *A Treatise on Human Nature*, J. M. Dent & Sons, 1952, vol. II, bk II, part I, section XI.

Benevolence and sympathy

The unsatisfactoriness of the notion of sympathy as an explanation of morality results from combining the ordinary meaning of the term with an additional element covering the mechanism through which self-love is transposed into the love of others. In its ordinary meaning sympathy is a moral emotion, which *presupposes* that we are morally related to those who evoke our sympathies. We must already perceive them to be ends of action for us, in order that our perception of their suffering should cause us to identify ourselves with that suffering, and to seek to relieve it. Sympathy, as Nagel says, is a 'pained awareness of their distress, *as something to be relieved*'.[50] Sympathy cannot, therefore, explain how we come to see their suffering as something to be relieved. It is merely the appropriate sentiment towards another, in his distress, whom we already treat as an end for us.

Yet it is precisely an explanation of how others come to be ends for us that the ethical doctrine of sympathy purports to provide. The elements of the explanatory claim are firstly, that the self-interested individual perceives other men as like himself, a suffering and pleasure-seeking being. At the very least, he perceives others as equally real as himself, as subjective beings concerned with their own interests. But, secondly, he is supposed to move from this perception of them to an association of their pain or pleasure with the idea of his own, and consequently to be disturbed or excited by it. And, thirdly the individual is supposed to be moved to action by this association to relieve or support the other. However, even if we grant that, through the association of the other's pain or pleasure with the idea of his own, the individual is disturbed, it must still be a matter for wonder why a hitherto purely self-interested being should consequently seek to relieve himself by relieving the distress of the other. The natural remedy for a self-interested being disturbed by the suffering of another would be to remove himself from the scene, and put the other out of his mind. And should the other's pleasure excite him, the natural response would not be pleasure at the other's pleasure, but a desire for

[50] T. Nagel, op. cit., p. 80 note 1.

53

the object that is the source of the other's enjoyment. At no point is there any plausible account of why an awareness of the other's suffering should transform a self-interested being into an other-interested one also.

It is evident that something is being presupposed in the argument that makes it appear plausible to those putting it forward to move from self-love, together with the recognition of the other as like oneself, to altruism. This must be something in the form which self-love takes in the first instance. If one's feeling for oneself takes an objective form so that one feels that one's suffering is something to be relieved by anyone, and one's pleasure something to be promoted by anyone, then it would follow from one's recognition that the other is a being like oneself that his suffering and pleasure have the same objective value as one's own. In seeing oneself in him one would feel his suffering as one's own. And this is the sentiment of sympathy. One acknowledges the claims on one of the other, not from self-interest or from rational principle, but from a feeling for oneself, which is, through the process of recognition, transposed into a feeling for the other.

This objective form of self-love, as I have argued above, itself requires justification and here obviously has none, since its presence is not even acknowledged. In fact it contains the moral principle implicitly within it, and so it is not surprising that the moral principle appears as a result. The moral principle is present in the form that human suffering as such is something to be relieved. But this principle evidently cannot be justified within the sympathy doctrine. The recognition of the presence in the argument of the objective form in which self-love is initially conceived must involve the supersession of the sympathy doctrine, and the attempt to justify the principle directly and not in terms of something else. This is to attempt a rationalist justification of morality.

ROUSSEAU

Although the notion of sympathy, as an explanation of the possibility of morality, is for the above reasons unsatisfactory, I shall now consider in more detail a thinker for whom sympathy or pity appears at times to serve as the basic relevant explanatory concept, namely Rousseau. However, his emphasis on pity is misleading. There is much more to his basic conceptions of the moral relation than the sympathy doctrine. In particular, we find in Rousseau an awareness of the necessity, in order to account for morality, of identifying and explaining a transformation of and re-ordering of the personality, from one governed by self-interested reason to one governed by moral reason. He recognizes that neither Hobbesian egoism nor the sympathy doctrine are adequate: egoism, because it is precisely the rejection of the necessity for such a transformation, and sympathy, because the difference between self-interested reason and moral reason is obscured by the presentation of the one as simply issuing from the other by a psychological mechanism. Rousseau contains rationalist elements within his thought, and reveals very clearly the self-division and opposition to which rationalism leads.

Rousseau, as everyone knows, believes that man is naturally good and corrupted only in society. The belief in natural goodness should involve a denial that an initial alienation of the individual from his relation to others is a necessary step in his attainment of a true moral relation to them. It would follow that the independent standpoint is not the standpoint for ethical thought, because the individual is naturally good for others. The alienation that is not inherent in the individual but produced by bad social arrangements can be overcome once and for all by good ones, so that successive generations will be naturally at one with their society. But this is not Rousseau's position. Consequently, much is missed in his thought if it is not grasped that, while he thinks that he is committed to the discovery of a conception of society which overcomes corruption once and for all, what he means by natural goodness and how he

55

understands the corruption of man in society ensures that alienation or corruption is a necessary element in man's social life, even in the new man in *Emile*, and the new society in the *Social Contract*. My claim is that there is in Rousseau's own conception of what he is doing a radical confusion.[51] To clarify the confusion is greatly to add to our understanding of the issues with which this work is concerned.

What might be called Rousseau's official view of his enterprise starts with the conception of a natural man who is an uncorrupted, undivided, harmonious but undeveloped whole, and proceeds through the idea of a social development of man which corrupts him, destroys his inner harmony and outer relations, and so creates self-division and opposition to others. The official project is, then, to conceive the conditions under which nature and society can be reconciled, and a new harmonious personality produced who is at one with himself and at one with others.[52] These conditions involve the development in the individual of a new moral personality and the attainment of a moral relation to others, through which there is an identity of interest of self and others. The official version purports to believe that this identity of interest ensures that the self-interest of the individual is fully satisfied at the same time as his common interest with others is brought into existence or given reality. Hence we have a harmony within each individual between his self-concern and moral personality and a harmony between individuals based on the interest that unites them.[53]

But this official version is contradicted by the profundity of insight revealed in his own analysis of the elements through which this project is to be realized. The crucial requirement for

[51] This may be said to be my third version of the incoherence in Rousseau's thought. See my book, *The Social Problem in the Philosophy of Rousseau*, Cambridge University Press, 1974; and my article, 'Rousseau and the Ideal of Community' in *History of Political Thought*, vol. 1, 1980. The three versions have basically the same structure and inspiration, but naturally I think the later versions show superior understanding to the earlier.

[52] See for instance the opening of *Emile*, *Oeuvres Complètes*, vol. 4, Bibliothèque de la Pléiade, p. 251.

[53] *The Social Contract*, Penguin Books, 1968, p. 75.

the realization of the project of a recovered harmony is that the moral good which unites one with others be fully integrated with self-love. And here Rousseau uses the sympathy doctrine to show how self-love transforms itself into a love of others. Since, on this view, altruism is derived from egoism, it is assumed that there cannot be any conflict between them. But Rousseau sees that the love of others based on sympathy or pity is not good enough for the moral relation, because, when it conflicts with the demands of our self-love, it will be defeated. Something more is required to provide a solid base for the moral relation. This is the point at which a new element committed to respect for the moral law is introduced, conscience. But since it is needed to subordinate the claims of self-love to one's unity with others, Rousseau cannot avoid recognizing the deep split in the personality that this new self creates. On the one hand the individual's virtue consists in a continuous self-combat, in which he imposes moral law on his private desires and on the other the citizen's virtue consists in a struggle to make his general will prevail over his private will. This self-division and opposition is the result of the emerging rationalist element in Rousseau's thought, namely the partial recognition that attachment to the moral law cannot in fact be derived from self-love and expressed in natural sentiments, but must be grounded in an independent principle.

Rousseau's argument can be reconstructed in three stages: (1) a notion of nature; (2) nature corrupted in bad social institutions into corrupt social man; (3) nature developed in good social institutions into moral man or the citizen.[54]

Natural man: For Rousseau the idea of natural man contains within it a conception of a good life, in terms of which the life of socially formed man can be judged to be corrupt. This element in the idea leads to serious difficulties. Firstly, since natural man is supposed to be a pre-social and pre-moral being,

---

[54] The first two stages correspond with Parts I and II of the *Discourse on Origins of Inequality*; the ethical stage includes *Emile* and the *Social Contract*.

the standard cannot be explicitly a moral one. Secondly, and more seriously, if natural man embodies in his life a standard for judging social man, natural man must be recognizably human. But the human being in Rousseau's thought, as for everybody in this tradition, is conceived as radically different from and essentially superior to the other animals, in that men are the loci of moral value. Thus a standard for judging a possible human life to be corrupt cannot be embodied in what is not a human life at all. Natural man must have human characteristics. But for the most part Rousseau presents him as a non-rational, impulsive or instinctive being; the distinctively human exists in nature only as a potential, to be developed in society.

I shall ignore this difficulty, and shall assume that natural man has sufficient of the human about him to do the crucial work that Rousseau demands of him. What is the standard that his life embodies? It is that of a self-dependent harmonious whole. Natural man is an isolated being, who is rarely in conflict with other members of his species, and even in such rare cases conflicts are temporary and of no moral significance. He is dependent on others neither materially nor mentally, but lives entirely in and for himself. In this sense his life can be said to be ordered wholly around himself. Of course, if he is a purely instinctive being, he cannot be understood to create or contribute to this order. It would be an order produced in him by his natural constitution, and he would not be self-dependent, because he would not be a self. But assuming that he is human and a self in some sense, we can say that what we have in the idea of natural man is the conception of a life, in which the individual himself and not something external to him is the source of the order in it, and in which a harmony reigns, both externally in respect of his environment, because there are no conflicts with others of any importance, and internally in respect of himself. Consequently he has to consider in ordering his life only himself, and not the claims of others. Rousseau's actual concept is, as I have indicated, both more complex and more confused than this, since it contains this idea of order as a *natural* order.

Nevertheless, it is this self-sufficient and harmonious whole which is shattered, once others enter into the individual's world in a permanent way both materially and mentally.

Before moving on to the next stage of corruption, I must say something about pity in natural man. Rousseau attributes to natural man two natural inclinations, self-love and pity. By pity Rousseau means a capacity to identify with suffering others. As mentioned above, Rousseau sees pity as the basis of the moral sentiment: morality is pity generalized to include all men. I shall discuss the role of pity in Rousseau's thought when the moralization of man is at issue. Here it should be noted that the attribution of pity to natural man raises, in an acute form, the question of the coherence of Rousseau's idea of natural man. For pity requires an orientation of the individual towards others, which the rest of his account of natural man as a self-dependent whole denies. Since the central idea to hold on to is that of natural man as self-dependent whole, let us suppose pity to be another of those undeveloped human potentialities in natural man.

Corrupt social man: The good of a self-dependent life is lost in the earliest societies, for men become dependent on each other both materially and mentally and as a result develop competitive and aggressive traits. The material or economic interdependence of men in society is an important part of Rousseau's account of corruption, but the really important dependence is at the level of mind. Men become concerned with the value other people give them. They no longer live in themselves, but in the judgements of others. In so far as the individual allows his actions to be determined by the evaluations of others, he ceases to be self-dependent, and his life becomes inauthentic. To be other-dependent, or dependent on something outside oneself, is now seen as an essential element in a bad or corrupt life, because it contradicts the idea that the source of value lies in the individual in his unmediated relation with himself.

We need to understand this two-fold characteristic of corrupt social man, aggressive competitiveness and dependence on the judgement of others. Aggressive competitiveness manifests itself in the drive for superiority over others. This involves many running the same race, and so being subject to the same set of evaluations. Why should self-dependent men in nature become these other-dependent competitors as soon as they enter into social relations? We must remember that the natural man who is being socialized into this aggressive, dependent creature is in nature governed only by self-love (assuming that pity is purely potential for development). In this respect, then, the idea of natural man involves a version of the independent standpoint, and the situation natural man is confronted with in society is that of having to pay attention to the claims of others. Rousseau's strategy here, however, is not to grapple immediately with the question, how natural man can be moralized, but instead he considers what would happen to this man were he to become dependent on others in a social existence. Although Rousseau's account of the corruption of natural man in society is intended as an historical reconstruction or hypothesis as to the essential elements in man's actual development, it can also be represented as an abstract thought-experiment in the above terms, which starts with the individual governed by self-love,[55] and considers what would happen to him as he enters into dependent social relations.

We know what Rousseau's answer to this question is: he would become an aggressive, dependent competitor. But how does he arrive at this answer? This is not at all clear, and we need to fill in Rousseau's account in order to show how the conclusion can be supposed to follow from the premises. Since we are starting with the individual occupying the independent standpoint, our first supposition will be that natural man's attitude to his own life is what I have called a subjective rather than an objective one. That is to say, in ordering his life, pursuing his desires, the values he attaches to his life is a value for himself only. (We must treat this attitude as implicit rather

[55] Self-love here is quite innocent, and so compatible with Rousseau's idea of natural goodness, precisely because of natural man's self-dependent existence.

than explicit in natural man's life, if we are to think of him as a natural instinctive being with the potential for having an attitude to his own life. What is implicit would, then, become explicit in society.) When this subjectively-oriented individual enters into social relations with others, he would no doubt come into conflict with similarly subjectively-oriented men, and so become competitors with them. But if he pursues self-interest in a purely subjective form, *he will have no interest in the valuations or judgements of him by others.* Yet this is the crucial fact about socialized natural man which produces his corrupt, aggressive behaviour. Hence one cannot move from the subjectivist view of natural man to the characteristics that he develops as corrupt, social man.

The alternative is to suppose that the implicit attitude that natural man has to his life is that it is of objective value. On this view, natural man in his isolated state prior to society treats his aims as implicitly values for anyone.[56] Since natural man knows no others, we would have to say that his attitude is implicitly such that, were there other valuers in existence, they would have to accept his valuations of his life as values for them also. Now this objectivist self-conception contains within itself two elements which, in an isolated existence, such as natural man's, are in harmonious unity. But the unity is contingent on this isolated life, and will be disrupted so soon as other valuers make their appearance in the objectivist individual's world. These two elements are, on the one hand, a subjective element consisting in the actual choices the individual makes in his life, considering only himself, and on the other the (implicit) objectivist principle that the choices of a self-forming being have objective value. Because in the state of nature each individual exists in a self-contained world, the only objective values each will confront will be those he himself creates.

What happens, then, when others erupt into his world and he becomes aware of other value-creators like himself? The two elements in his nature *could* come into conflict. The objective

---

56 Consider that this is, in effect, Gewirth's account of what is involved in human agency.

side *should* lead him to acknowledge these other beings as of equal worth with himself, and their subjective choices as values for everyone. But this would require him to separate off his objective side from its immediate but contingent unity with his subjective side, and limit his subjective choices by respect for the equal worth of all as value-creators. This is evidently not the course that socialized natural man pursues on Rousseau's hypothesis. It is, indeed, what he *should* do, and Rousseau in *Emile* and the *Social Contract* gives us an account of what is required to produce this course. In the *Discourse on Inequality*, however, Rousseau's hypothesis can be represented in this way: the individual tries to preserve his natural unity (of subjective and objective elements) in society by making other valuers conform their value judgements to his own, and become the slavish endorsers of his own view of himself. This would, if successful, preserve his natural unity, since, while there appear to be other creators around, in fact they are made into mere replicators of his own creative activity. His aim is to secure from them the recognition of his primacy, and the non-independence of themselves as creators of value. This strategy, however, leads the individual into contradictions; on the one hand he seeks a judgement from others, and thus becomes dependent on them for the sense of his existence, and on the other hand, the fact that the content of the judgement that he seeks is the recognition of his primacy leads him into a struggle to assert his superiority over them and dominate them. Here, then, we have the two-fold characteristic of Rousseau's socially corrupted man, dependence on others in the sense of living in their judgements, and aggressive competitiveness essentially concerned with establishing dominance. The incoherence of this strategy consists in the impossibility of obtaining from others the recognition which the individual seeks. The corruption consists in the inauthenticity of living outside oneself in the opinions of others, as well as in the straightforward evil of the struggle for domination.

Natural man moralized: Emile: According to Rousseau the actual history of man is to be understood as reflecting the adoption by men of something like the above strategy. It is obvious that other elements are necessary to make human society possible at all, but rather than consider these, consider Rousseau's first account of the way out of this impasse in *Emile*.

Emile is to be educated until adolescence without, if possible, acquiring any moral conceptions of his relations to others. He is described as being at adolescence alone in the world, dependent on no-one, living like natural man in himself, not in the judgements of others.[57] With adolescence it is necessary for him to come to terms with others, and this is the point at which he will either be corrupted in the manner described above or, avoiding that strategy, will successfully acquire a moral character. Here again we are presented with an instance of the independent, non-moralized individual confronted with the question of how he is to stand in relation to the claims of others. It is now that Rousseau gives his account of the possibility of morality. The moral problem, as Rousseau describes it at this point, is how, despite the fact that we naturally put ourselves first, we can come to love others as ourselves, i.e. recognize the equal worth of others.[58] His answer, in the first place, is that pity sets us going in the right direction. We have to learn to identify ourselves with another so that the other and ourselves constitute a unity. Pity produces this, since in pitying we identify ourselves with the suffering other, and feel his desires as our own. We act for him for the love of ourselves. Pity thus contains the central requirement of the moral relation, but produces it only in particular cases. To create the full moral attitude it is necessary to generalize pity to cover man as such.

If Rousseau's corrupted social man is to be understood as the product of objective individualism,[59] then one ought, in these terms, to be able to account for Rousseau's conception of the emergence of moral man also. One can do so in this way: the objective individualist, adopting the corrupt strategy, implicitly demands that in respect of others he should always be the first,

[57] Rousseau, *Oeuvres Complètes*, vol. 4, p. 484.
[58] ibid., p. 523 and note.
[59] The claim that the individual's choices are values for any one.

indeed the only one, that counts. The alternative strategy is that of equality, through which the objective individualist recognizes that, since others are like himself, they have as much claim to value as himself, and hence must be of equal worth. The necessary condition for arriving at this position is the recognition that others are like oneself. Pity is for Rousseau the means whereby this necessary requirement is first satisfied.[60] But seeing others as like oneself only produces the desired result if the individual is implicitly adopting the objectivist position in respect of his own life. As I have argued before, if he is adopting a subjective attitude to his own life, he can recognize others as like himself without attributing any value to them for him. Thus the pity or sympathy account of the possibility of morality assumes a principle that it does not justify; and since this principle is implicitly the moral principle of the inherent worth of self-determining beings, the pity or sympathy explanation cannot be other than a superficial one.

Rousseau emphasizes strongly that morality involves the transference of self-love into the love of others. This is like the Hobbesian position in so far as it assimilates the requirements of morality to the love of self, but it does this not by affirming that morality is simply a refined form of self-love, but by the transference mechanism of pity or sympathy, which converts self-love into morality. This type of explanation tends to obscure the difference between self-love and morality, and if Rousseau had remained content with it, he would not have prepared the way for the rationalist theory of Kant. It is the more surprising that he did not remain content with it, in that it offers a way of conceiving of the desired unity in society between oneself and others. If through pity one loves others as oneself, it would seem necessary only to discover the conditions under which pity can come to prevail in one's relations with others.

In saying that Rousseau did not remain content with the pity explanation of morality, I do not mean that he came to reject it; he found it insufficient and added to it. The additional element

[60] ibid., p. 503.

is divine conscience, which he conceives as an innate sentiment impelling us to the love of justice, or the love of others as ourselves. This innate sentiment is not at all a sentiment of benevolence which explains our impulse to a concern for others. The divine conscience comes into force only when through the rational development of pity we have an intellectual grasp of the basic principle of justice. Conscience explains not how we arrive at the principle, but why we feel compelled to pursue it *against our natural inclinations*. And here with the introduction of conscience we come to the recognition that the love of justice and the love of self are quite distinct and opposed principles in man, making him in his earthly existence an irremediably divided being. To achieve moral virtue, and hence be good for others, is not to create a new whole which incorporates one's own interest and the interest of others in an harmonious moral union; it is to commit oneself to an incessant self-combat to ensure that one's moral conscience will prevail over one's natural self-love.[61]

This new element specifically opposes morality to self-love, and thus contradicts their apparent assimilation in the pity theory. This does not lead Rousseau to reject the assimilating version; for we find him returning to it from time to time. As a result he has two versions of the relation of self-love and the moral principle, in one of which they are harmonized. It is the retention of this version that allows him to continue to suggest that, at any rate, in his political ideal of the *Social Contract*, the new harmonious whole is possible.

In the above account there is a puzzle as to why Rousseau comes to find pity an insufficient explanation of morality, and why he seeks a further underpinning for it in conscience. I think that the answer must lie in the equivocation which his basic claim of man's natural goodness and social corruption contains. As noted, it implies that a new social whole is possible without corruption. Yet man's natural goodness amounts in the end simply to the *absence* of both good and bad emotions in his natural condition. Furthermore, it is not in the end bad social

[61] ibid., pp. 583–606.

arrangements, private property and division of labour, which corrupts man, but the strategy he is naturally inclined to take up when faced with his fellow men. From this it must follow that man in society is inherently inclined to corruption, and that unity with others is only possible by developing in man a potentiality for morality which can be brought to oppose and dominate that inclination.

This separate development of the moral side of man and its opposition to self-interest can also be understood in terms of the distinction between subjective and objective elements in the individual. The subjective side is the individual's will in so far as he is concerned with making choices for his own life. The objective side is the will affirming that the authentic choices of subjectively oriented particular wills have moral worth. Developed as a moral will, it affirms this as true not just for its own particular will, but for all men. The moral will in an individual thus ceases to be immediately united with that individual's particular will. It values other particular wills as much as its own, and this concern with equality brings it into a potential conflict with the individual's own particular will. For the particular will remains concerned with authentic choices for its own separate life. Yet such choices must also accord with the claims of others enforced by the individual's own moral will. Since there is no reason to suppose a harmony between the authentic choices of each man's particular will, their conflict will appear also as conflict within the individual between his 'natural' or original inclination to give preference to himself, and his moral conscience's demand to value all equally.

The conflict between these two wills in Rousseau's thought can be easily perceived in his political theory.

The citizen: Rousseau's political community is created through a contract which brings into existence a general will. I take this general will and the relation it involves to be an instantiation in a particular collection of men of the moral will discussed above. In that case the bond uniting the citizens would be the abstract conception of the value that each has in himself, and it might be thought that in his political theory Rousseau presents a concrete conception of the individual's value in terms of his membership of a larger whole. It is true that the value that individuals have for each other is created through a contract among a particular collection of men, but what determines whether the conception of value is an abstract individualist one of the kind under analysis in Part I of this work or not is the nature of the commitment that is involved in the contract. And it is clear that contractants are committed to being bound by rules which treat each *individual* of equal worth with others. This means that by the terms of the contract each is committed to treating the others as having value as individuals in themselves. This is disguised by the fact that it is apparently only as members of a community that they have value for each other. The truth is that a political community is a way of bringing moral value into existence in relations between men. The community recognizes the value that resides in each individual.

There is once again the problem of deriving the equality principle, which is the basis of a valid political community, from individuals in a state of nature or independent position. Rousseau's derivation is hardly very clear. But it appears to be founded on a common interest that underlies and unites all the different self-interests of men.[62] It is an equality of right that is derived from the preference which each gives himself and so from the nature of man, with the result that each in working for others is working for himself and in voting for the good of all thinks of himself.[63] On this view of the nature of the bond

---

[62] Rousseau distinguishes between the will of all and the general will. The former is a sum of particular wills, the latter is a will for the common good. But he tells us that if we take away from the particular wills the 'pluses and minuses that cancel each other out, the sum of the difference will be the general will' (*The Social Contract*, Penguin Books, pp. 72–3). I take this to mean that the natural direction of the particular will is to desire restraints on others from which the individual himself is absolved. If all these self-preferences are cancelled out, we are left with rules which constrain all equally and such is the nature of the general will. If the general will is to be implicit in particular wills seeking their own advantage, it must once again be the case that the particular will takes the form of objective egoism. [63] *The Social Contract*, p. 75.

which unites the citizens there should be no conflicting interests, but only a harmony of justice and self-interest.

This is only half of Rousseau's story. The other half involves the recognition of the fragility of the bond which unites citizens, and the necessity for a powerful element of sentiment, patriotism, to help them affirm their unity over and against their conflicting interests. For he now admits that the newly emergent general will is founded in opposition to all particular wills,[64] that particular wills and general wills tend in opposite directions, one to equality and the other to self-preference,[65] and that the community is in constant danger of being undermined by the conflict of particular interests.[66] All this derives from the fact that the foundation of the general will in the objective element of the natural individual causes the division within the individual between this objective will and his empirical will for his own interests. The former is the foundation for the love of other persons as oneself, but as such is opposed to the love of the latter for itself alone. If each person or citizen has a general will which unites him with others, as a man he has a particular will which can be contrary to his general will.[67] This disunity in the midst of apparent harmony tends to be concealed from us and from Rousseau himself by the emphasis which he gives in his writing to the level at which interests are united and citizens are one – the general or purely political level. If citizens can in respect of their particular life be kept apart as much as possible (they should be, he says, as little dependent on each other as possible),[68] and if they can be brought together only in the political realm in which nothing but common interests are noted and celebrated, the inherent disunity underlying the political realm can be to a certain extent neglected or ignored.[69]

[64] ibid., note to 73.
[65] ibid., p. 69.
[66] ibid., p. 150.
[67] ibid., p. 63.
[68] ibid., p. 99.
[69] In his essay on the Jewish Question Marx identifies Rousseau's thought with the attempt to emancipate man in a purely political way, and correctly sees that this involves a radical separation of the private man from the citizen with the result that man's communal life is located in a political realm

RATIONALISM AND KANT

Rousseau's view of conscience as the impulse which makes morality possible separates the moral impulse from self-love and as a necessary consequence opposes them to each other. This view has the great merit that it fully recognizes the necessity for the subordination of self-interested reason to moral reason, and hence the necessity, for this to be possible, for the emergence in man of a new personality, whether this is the purely moral man of *Emile*, or the citizen of the *Social Contract*, which is capable of taking control of the individual and subjecting his self-interest to its demands. As we have seen, Rousseau does not carry this programme through, but equivocates on the relation of self-love and morality. Rationalism, here, is to be understood as the view which does carry through the implications of Rousseau's notion of conscience as a self-motivating moral idea. It is the view that if morality is to be possible, moral reason must motivate of itself, without being dependent on self-interest or any sentiment of benevolence or sympathy. Kant is the theorist who worked out most fully in individualist terms what must be the case if moral reason is to constitute its own motive.

The central conviction of Kant's ethical view is that the only thing that is good in itself is the good will, and the good will is that will which aims at realizing the morally good for its own sake, not as a means to anything else. Duty must be done for duty's sake.[70] The problem of Kant's ethics is that of showing how this good will is possible.

By the notion of the will Kant means practical reason or thought controlling and directing impulse and desire in the form of maxims or policies. Intelligent willed action is in the first place action whose motive is an interest guided by an

that is opposed to his real empirical life. Of course Marx neglects the other half of Rousseau's story; perhaps because he intends to realize its aspirations. See D. McLellan (ed.), *Karl Marx: Early Texts*, Basil Blackwell, 1971, pp. 107–8.

[70] *Fundamental Principles of the Metaphysic of Ethics*, Longman, 1962, pp. 10–16.

appropriate conception. But while reason is in this way practical, it is nevertheless empirically determined, for it guides action within the system of natural impulses and desires and with a view to the satisfaction of such desires in however rationalized a form.[71] If the good will is to exist, then we must have a conception of practical reason which is not determined in the above way by anything external to itself, or in other words we need the idea of a reason that determines to action of itself, and this would be a pure practical reason.

The conception of a pure practical reason is the idea of a categorical imperative. In all practical principles we can distinguish the form that principles have from their matter or content. Thus, for Kant, all practical principles have the form of imperatives; they command what a person who acknowledges the principle ought to do, and hence the form is, you ought to do X, where X represents the matter or content of the principle. When practical reason is not pure but empirical (not self-determinant but externally determined), practical principles are conditional imperatives; they command only conditionally upon the agent's acceptance of the end that the principle is directed to realizing. A pure practical reason, if it is to exist, must contain an unconditional imperative and so must command categorically. Since all practical principles whose validity depends on their content are conditional, a categorical imperative must command independently of its content, and that means in respect of its form only. It will have to command in virtue only of its having the form of an imperative. This form is that of a pure ought or the pure idea of a law. The categorical imperative is: 'Act only on that maxim whereby thou canst at the same time will that it should become a universal law.'[72] Where does the universal element in the categorical imperative come from? The pure idea of a law is that of a law that commands unconditionally, that is to say independently of anything else whatsoever, and hence commands universally or without qualification.

[71] Kant, *Critique of Practical Reason*, Longman, 1959, pp. 107–14.
[72] Kant, *Fundamental Principles*, p. 46.

If pure reason is to be practical, then the individual must be capable of being determined to action by the idea of a universal law alone. This categorical imperative has in itself no content and some substantive content is necessary if men are to be guided by law to action. The substantive content cannot be derived from the empty pure form and Kant's idea is that it can be derived through bringing subjective or empirically determined maxims to the bar of the categorical imperative, and those that pass the test of universalization are thereby demonstrated to be universally valid and substantive moral laws. On this view the validity of the maxim is determined by its universal form alone, so that the laws can be said to be the product of pure reason and the individual in being governed by them can be said to be determined by pure practical reason.

It is essential for Kant's project that the substantive moral laws be the product of pure reason. Consider some of his examples of the deduction of such laws:

1 The subjective maxim is that out of self-love I propose to make deceitful promises when in difficulty. Kant's claim is that if this maxim were to be universalized, it would destroy itself, since, were everyone to act on this law, there would quickly be an end to the practice of promising. Universalizing the maxim makes it self-contradictory, and hence rules it out.[73] In this way its converse becomes a substantive moral law.

2 The subjective maxim is never to help another in distress. Here Kant argues that while such a universal law might exist as a law of nature, viz. that no-one does help another in distress, because the species can survive through self-help, yet it is impossible for an individual to will such a law. Such a will would contradict itself, 'inasmuch as many cases might occur in which one would have need of the love and sympathy of others, and in which by such a law of nature sprung from his own will, he would deprive himself of all hope of the aid he desires'.[74]

[73] ibid., pp. 23 and 47–8.   [74] ibid., p. 49.

Kant gives other examples concerning suicide and the neglect of one's talents but in these two the principles involved can be seen clearly enough here.

In the first case, where would be the self-contradiction in willing the disappearance of the practice of promising? There is only self-contradiction if one both wills the practice of promising and at the same time wills the lying promise maxim. But it is not pure reason that tells one to will the practice of promising: the desirability of the practice is not derived from the pure idea of law. Hence the deduction fails. In the second example it is even more obvious that one can will without self-contradiction that no-one be helped when in distress including oneself. The contradiction derives from the presumed initial wish of one's own to be helped in distress, which conflicts with the will universalized that no-one help another. But since this initial will cannot be derived from the pure idea of universal law, once again the deduction fails.

Leaving aside the question of the derivability of the moral laws from pure reason by the criterion of universalizability, and considering the criterion itself as used by Kant and subsequent moral philosophers, it is clear that it is intended as a necessary and sufficient condition of valid moral law. For this to be at all plausible, however, the initial subjective maxim must be of a certain sort. Mackie[75] in a recent book distinguishes three possible stages of universalization: (1) at the first stage it is only the numerical difference between one person and another that is ruled out by the requirement to universalize. The difference in treatment between me and others cannot be grounded simply in the fact that I am I and not the others. There must be some substantial difference justifying any differential treatment. But this allows for any substantial difference to count, as the differentiating ground, viz. race, colour etc. and so a second stage of universalization is required to eliminate this unjust discrimination. (2) This involves universalizing while putting yourself in the other person's position, e.g. suppose you were yellow, would you like race discrimination against yellows? The idea is

[75] J. L. Mackie, *Ethics*, Penguin Books, 1977, ch. 4.

that maxims be resolved upon from a standpoint which eliminates differences of mental and physical qualities. But this position is reached only if the individual's initial maxims are of an 'individualist' nature. Thus the race 'fanatic' will certainly not be moved by putting himself into the yellow race's shoes, since his supreme value is not the individual at all but the race. (3) Mackie's third stage is supposed to take account of different tastes and rival ideals, which the second stage does not do, since it eliminates (supposedly) only qualities of the agent, not qualities of his will. This stage involves voting for maxims from a standpoint which is quite independent of any particular quality of the agent whatsoever, including tastes and ideals. Here we have arrived at the notion of the pure individual agent choosing maxims, which is to say that the individual chooses as though he were anyone.[76] The fundamental principle to which they will agree in these circumstances is the equal value of persons as agents. The universalizability requirement is thus another way of affirming the modern individualist moral principle. But it works only if we start with individuals who claim objective value for their own aims and desires and do not immediately extend such value to others. That such individuals are involved in self-contradiction by this denial follows from the fact that the value they accord to themselves must be grounded in their pure individuality, and this value must be equally present in others. The individual is already committed to the universal principle in his initial egoism. But none of this follows if on the one hand the individual's initial position is one of subjective egoism, or if on the other hand other than individualist values are affirmed.

Does Kant's use of the universalizability criterion follow this pattern? Yes. Kant's examples work only if he is implicitly assuming that the subjective maxims which have to be universalized are of an objective egoist nature. Thus the maxim I will never help another in distress results in self-contradiction when given the universal form, no-one is to help another in distress,

---

[76] Compare this with Rawls's requirement that individuals choose principles of justice from behind a veil of ignorance, Rawls, op. cit., p. 136.

because the individual is nevertheless committed to the maxim that *he* ought to be helped in distress. Similarly the lying promise maxim is incoherent because the individual wishes to attach a value to his actions which he denies to other identical agents. Universalizing the maxim simply brings out the incoherence of attaching a universal value to the single ego. In any case Kant makes this argument explicitly: he says 'Man necessarily conceives his own existence as being so [an end in itself]: so far, then, this is a subjective principle of human actions. But every other rational being regards its existence similarly, just on the same rational principle that holds for me; so that it is at the same time an objective principle, from which as a supreme practical law, all laws of the will must be capable of being deduced.'⁷⁷ The argument goes thus: (1) Each individual treats his existence as for himself an end in itself, i.e. of absolute or objective worth. (2) Every other does also, and hence rational nature is an end in itself, or an end for everyone. If we re-phrase the argument in a clearer way, it goes thus: (1) Each individual treats his existence as an end in itself and thus an end for anyone. (2) He cannot claim objective worth for his rational existence unless he allows the same worth to any other rational being. Here each treats rational nature as an objective end *in his own person*, and so cannot deny it in others without self-contradiction. It is this initial objective attitude to one's own existence that gives universalizing a moral effectiveness. Of course, once again it needs to be said that Kant is simply wrong in holding that man *necessarily* conceives his existence as an end in itself. For he can conceive it, and must initially do so, simply as an end for himself, an end of purely subjective worth, from which universalizing fails to produce a moral conclusion.

On the above arguments Kant's aim of describing substantial moral maxims which are pure practical laws cannot succeed. But allowing him the derivation of these laws from pure reason, consider the problem of motivation. The motive for acting in accordance with these laws cannot be anything other than pure respect for the law or in other words respect for the pure form

⁷⁷ Kant, *Fundamental Principles*, p. 56.

of law, its universal nature. Otherwise we would not have an instance of *pure* practical reason, but of practical reason ultimately determined by some non-rational desire or impulse. How can the individual be determined to action by pure respect for the law? Clearly this question, if it refers to the individual as an empirical self-interested being, has no answer. For the moral motive to exist, there must exist another, purely rational self with ends entirely different from those of the individual as empirical being. Kant holds that if the categorical imperative is to be possible, we need the notion of an end of action which is an objective end, an end of absolute worth, and proceeds to the affirmation that: 'Man and generally any rational being exists as an end in himself, not merely as a means to be arbitrarily used by this or that will.'[78] The foundation of the pure practical principle is that 'rational nature exists as an end in itself'.[79]

The notion of rational nature as an end in itself would seem to be the notion that the end of a rational being is to develop or give actuality to its own rational nature. Pure reason is given such actuality in men when men's actions are determined by the pure reason in them. In this way pure rational law is actualized in men's lives. Such a rational will in men will be a self-legislating one since it gives the law to itself: the law is its own nature issuing forth. Kant also describes this will as autonomous, since it is a law to itself.[80] But all this elaboration of the characteristics of the moral will continues to beg the question. At most it shows what must be the case if morality or pure practical reason is to be possible. It does not show that morality is possible, for it does not show that man is a purely rational being.

To show this we need to establish that man's will is free in an absolute sense, that it is free of all determination other than that of its own nature: its determination consists in its self-determination. Kant cannot possibly be satisfied with the view of free will as thought-mediated action, where this mediation may itself comprise part of a system of causal laws. This would be the relative freedom of empirical practical reason and quite

[78] ibid., p. 55.   [79] ibid., p. 56.   [80] ibid., p. 171.

insufficient to ground morality. The Kantian view requires the will to be an absolutely independent source of action in the world. What is Kant's argument for the existence of an absolutely free will? In a sense his whole work on both theoretical and practical reason can be seen as an attempt to show that the idea of free will is a necessary postulate of reason. In the ethics the proof he offers first is that a rational being which has a will cannot act except under the idea of freedom, and this shows that in a practical point of view the will really is free. For in so far as the rational being acts thinking himself to be free, and thus on the basis of a universal law, then he must really be free, for he could not otherwise have acted on the law.[81] But once again this merely shows that if there are rational beings with a will, they must be free. It does not show that such beings exist or that men are rational beings.

Indeed Kant admits that we cannot prove freedom to be actually a property of ourselves or of human nature. But he holds that we must presuppose this freedom, if we would conceive of a rational being endowed with a will. This, Kant also admits, seems to involve moving in a circle. We assume absolute freedom in order to explain the possibility of a pure rational will, and assume a pure rational will in order to explain the possibility of absolute freedom.[82]

At this point in his ethics he has recourse to his arguments on the nature of theoretical reason, and some attention must be given to them.[83] His aim is to show that the existence of man as a purely rational being, and hence absolutely free, is a necessary postulate of theoretical reason, and thus that *quite independently of our experience of morality*, there is warrant for our belief in the possibility of freedom. The initial distinction from which his argument takes off is that between objects as they appear to us and are known by us and objects as they are apart from how they affect us and so as they are in themselves. From this it follows that behind the appearances of

---

[81] ibid., pp. 80–1.   [82] ibid., p. 83.
[83] ibid., pp. 84 ff., a summary, of course, of the arguments of the *Critique of Pure Reason*.

things to us are the things in themselves, which as such we can never know. This distinction applies to man himself. The knowledge that we have of ourselves is of how we appear to ourselves as phenomena. But we must suppose something else to be the basis of these phenomena, the ego or self as it is in itself. The thing in itself Kant calls the noumenal. Man is a dual being, phenomenal and noumenal. As phenomenal being he is part of a world of sense, but as noumenal being he is part of an intellectual world about which we can have no further knowledge.

We can have no knowledge of things as they are in themselves, yet rational belief about them is possible. These beliefs are ideas of reason, and reason is a special faculty, distinct from that of the understanding, a faculty of systematic thought whereby we aim at a system of complete knowledge. Reason is the faculty which drives us on always to go beyond any given and limited explanation of the world provided by the faculty of understanding, and seeks the explanation of that explanation, until we arrive at an explanation that has no condition, but is itself the unconditioned condition of all conditional explanations. This drive of reason for the absolute and complete explanation cannot be satisfied within the categories of experience through which we have knowledge of the world. So reason is forced to go beyond experience to think super-sensible realities. These are ideas of reason, or postulates necessary to make sense of the world of understanding and experience. Freedom is one such idea. It is the idea of a free or unconditioned cause, and Kant's claim is that this is a possible idea if we take it to apply to the noumenal world and not to the phenomenal world. In the phenomenal world the principle of causality, that every event has a cause, applies universally, but reason demands that there must be a cause which itself has no cause, if the succession of causes in the phenomenal world is to be intelligible. Applying these ideas to man's moral experience, we get the view that as noumenal ego man is not part of the world of causal determination. As such a being belonging to a purely intelligible world man must think himself to be independent of causality, and hence to be an absolutely free will. Yet as a phenomenal being man is subject to causality and cannot be free. This is not a contradiction, Kant claims, because freedom and determination apply to man as different beings.

This argument presupposes a certain conception of the faculty of reason, namely that it is a drive to find the Absolute, which entails that ideas of free causes, among other ideas, will be necessary to satisfy it. But, besides this, Kant admits that the faculty of reason establishes only a necessary hypothesis, and cannot explain how freedom is possible. 'Freedom is a mere Idea or Ideal Conception, the objective reality of which can in no wise be shown according to laws of nature, and consequently not in any possible experience, and for this reason can never be comprehended or understood.'[84] It follows also that the question as to how a categorical imperative is possible can be answered only by assigning the one hypothesis on which it is possible, namely the idea of freedom, and by discerning the necessity of this hypothesis. 'But to explain how pure reason can be of itself practical without the aid of any spring of action that could be derived from any other source. . .is beyond the power of human reason.'[85] After all these manoeuvres we are not finally left with the understanding of how morality is possible, but the comprehension of its incomprehensibility.[86]

This must be admitted to be a defeat. Kant, after all his intellectual labour, has shown that if we are committed to the view that morality requires an independent moral motive, then we shall also have to commit ourselves to other beliefs which even so do not in the end succeed in explaining the possibility of the independent moral motive. One of the reasons for this failure consists in the necessity to conceive of man as radically divided being, both free and determined, a being of pure reason and a being of desire. A harmonization of these two beings in man, some way in which they can be brought into relation with one another, is obviously necessary for an intelligible conception of man, morality and freedom. For one thing, if one and the same act is both free, as the product of man's noumenal

[84] ibid., p. 95.   [85] ibid., p. 99.   [86] ibid., p. 102.

being, and determined, as the product of his phenomenal being, it must be the case that the drive of free will and the aim of desire bring about the same result. Otherwise the same act could not conceivably be both free and determined. In ethical terms Kant has the idea of such a union in his notion of a Kingdom of Ends.[87] This is a union of several rational beings in a system of common laws, in which all ends, both the objective ends that each has as a rational being, and the special subjective ends that each proposes to himself as a particular being, are combined in a systematic and harmonious whole. Each is both end and means to the other, so that each realizes his special private ends by means of the others, while respecting the other as an end in himself. This is another idea of reason or Ideal Conception. But if a rational being necessarily aims at this ideal in his action, while at the same time his action is determined on quite other principles, i.e. by desire, then we must ask whether the world is already ideal or not. If it is not, then we are faced with the gross absurdity of a man endowed with free will which is helpless over and against his empirical will.

Kant's way out of this is to produce as another idea of reason a teleological conception of nature and history,[88] according to which the necessary union of free will and natural determination is a process built into the structure of the world to be approached in the course of history. On this view we must conceive of nature as though it existed for some end, and of that end as the realization of rational nature. Nature, as the faculty of the understanding conceives it, is a succession of phenomena linked by causal laws. But our minds cannot be satisfied with such a conception for we are driven to ask for a purpose which lies behind and makes intelligible to us this system of laws. Hence we must think of the system of nature as an overall self-unfolding teleological process, a process that is developing itself towards a final goal. This final goal can only be the full development of man's capacities as a rational being.

[87] ibid., p. 62.
[88] To be found in respectively *The Critique of Judgement* and *The Idea for a Universal History with a Cosmopolitan Purpose.*

For the only goal of absolute worth, as we have seen, is rational being. Man is the only rational being in nature, hence nature must have man in his rational aspect as its final end. Otherwise nature has no end, but is a thing in vain.

If we accept this conception, then it follows that man as *a natural being* will be acting in accordance with his nature in such a way as to bring about in the course of history the conditions for the realization of the pure moral will. It is man's unsocial sociability, man's inclination to live together with others, while striving to live as an individual in accordance with how *he* wants to live, that is the driving force in this process. The resulting antagonism within society leads to the development of men's talents, which in the end can transform 'a pathologically enforced social union into a moral whole'.[89]

These ideas of nature and history are again only necessary postulates of reason. They do not constitute knowledge, and may be said to add further to the list of assumptions that have to be made about the nature of the world if the idea of the moral will understood in rationalist terms is to be intelligible. They are attempts to show what must be thought, if absolute freedom is to be possible. The story, at this point, leads naturally on to Kant's successors, the German Idealists. But these, in order to establish Kant's case, find it necessary to abandon his individualist premises, and thus turn themselves into critics of individualism rather than its supporters. Hegel's version of this development I will consider in Part II.

Teleological conceptions of nature and history are required to provide an intelligible account of the harmonious union of noumenal and phenomenal worlds, which overcomes the apparently hopelessly divided nature of man. Do they succeed? Not in Kant's case, in so far as he remains an individualist. For in so far as his argument purports to show how through the operation of man's unsocial sociability a social arrangement is produced which coincides with the commands of pure reason, he has not shown that a moral will is actual in man. He has

[89] H. Reiss (ed.), *Kant's Political Writings*, Cambridge University Press, 1971, p. 45.

shown only the existence of an extraordinary and as yet incomprehensible coincidence of natural interest and reason. If a rational will is to be actual, it must produce the result, the perfect social arrangement, by itself explicitly determining men's actions in their conscious willing of a rational end. But it cannot do this except by being causally efficient in the same world as the phenomenal nature of man. Yet this coexistence of natural and rational will on the same level would immediately re-establish the impossible opposition between them. Thus reason can be understood to determine the result only by operating behind the scenes as the inner purpose of the whole process of natural determination, and this idea fails to show how the absolutely free rational will can be actual in man.

SELF-INTEREST, MORALITY
AND THE DIVIDED SELF

In these critical accounts of the explanations of the possibility of morality in Hobbes, Rousseau and Kant, the movement of thought has been from the attempt to identify morality with self-interest, either in the form of egoism or in that of sympathy, to a recognition of the incongruity between the two and the necessary subordination of the one to the other. But this advance required a conception of the independent motivational structure of moral reason, which succeeded only in developing a conception of an impossibly divided self, and a demand for the reconciliation once more of self-interest and morality in a philosophy of history. That is to say, the movement of thought reveals that rationalism is the implicit truth of the earlier conceptions, and in bringing out the truth contained in them, it makes explicit the radical division of the two levels of the self that is implicit in individualist ethics.

The divided self is the consequence of the conception of the value of the individual's particular life as lying in an unmediated relation to himself. Implicit in the modern doctrine is the view that the individual's particular choices for his life are morally valid only if they are authentic expressions of his own will; but at the same time this view requires that the individual's choices for his life do not detract from the equal value that inheres in other individuals.

Thus, there are two criteria for the objective worth of an individual's particular interests, and they can produce a conflict of objective values. What an individual desires for himself authentically may be irretrievably frustrated by some state of the world legitimately enjoyed by others. If there is no reason to suppose that the authentic particular desires of men will spontaneously harmonize with each other, and so harmonize with the common interest between them, through which they recognize their equal value for each other, then there always exists a potential conflict within the individual between the right of the particular self to its authentic self-realization and the objective requirement to respect the rights of others. And so we would have an intolerably divided self. It is for this reason that modern ethical thought shows so strong a need to reconcile the demands of self-interest and the requirements of morality. It is this need which gives an overall sense to the apparently absurd enterprise of Hobbes of presenting morality as an extension of self-interest, and is met with again at the other extreme in Kantianism when it compels Kant in his philosophy of history into the un-Kantian position of showing how self-interest supports morality.

The determining factor in the creation of this unacceptable potential split between self-interest and morality, or as one can say particular and common interest, consists in the requirement that to be authentic the individual's choice of his particular life must be determined having only himself as his end, and so independently of any relation to others in which they constitute ends for him. This requirement ensures that the content of the individual's particular will must be determined *independently* of the demands of morality. This brings about the separate existence of the two levels, particular and common or general. On the one hand, authenticity cannot allow the individual in his particular choices to have another as an end for him, since this will give the other a power to determine the particular worth of the individual's life: on the other hand, morality requires that others be accepted as ends. The only way to combine these two demands is to seek to fulfil them on separate and independent levels.

In so far as others are ends for one, they must be ends in abstraction from their particular choices and lives, and independently of any relation to one's own particular life. They are ends as *pure* agents or choosers, in complete abstraction from all particularity. Because they are such ends, each has to value the others' particular choices, but only as an endorsement of the others' authentic choice for their lives. As a valuer of the others' particular lives, one is oneself a pure moral being, abstracted from one's own particularity. By thus abstracting the moral from the particular, it is possible formally to combine the demand both to have, and not to have, others as one's end. It is this identification of the other as an end in abstraction from both his and one's own particularity, and so in abstraction from any relation between particular lives, which constitutes the essential element in modern individualist ethical thought. If a more satisfactory ethical theory is to be arrived at, this process of abstraction must be avoided.

Because on that theory the moral and the particular dimensions of individual and social life are independently identified and determined, it follows that they are by their natures opposed to each other. The one directs the individual to a pure self-concern, and the other to a pure valuation of others as equals. Thus when the moral law conflicts with authentic particular desire, the individual as a particular cannot authentically pay any attention to that law. But morality does not have any purchase on the content of particular willing either. For since the essence of morality is this abstract valuation of selves, and the moral self is the pure abstract valuer of particular lives, it is itself necessarily empty of all particular content. In its affirmation of the moral law against the individual's own particular will, it cannot alter the content of that will except by altering the calculation of self-interest by which that will is determined, so as to make independent self-interest and morality coincide again. But how is this to be done? If the world is not already ideal, or if it does not have the production of the ideal programmed into it, the conscious moral will cannot bring about the necessary alterations.

The potential conflict between particular and moral wills depends entirely on the existence of a conflict between the particular interests or values different individuals pursue. If these were spontaneously harmonized, the rights of others would necessarily not be infringed. But then there would be no role for the moral will to play: it would be a mere ghostly onlooker in the natural harmony of the world. If men's particular values do spontaneously conflict, and who is there so absurd as to deny this, there is no way of harmonizing them that does not infringe somebody's right.

My claim is that rationalism makes fully explicit the nature of this divided self. It does so by demonstrating the impossibility of establishing an identity of self-interest and morality, and hence by showing that, if morality is to be possible on individualist premises, the individual must be governed by a purely rational will quite independently of self-interest. For the implicit opposition between the particular and moral dimensions of individual life is concealed in the pre-rationalist theories by the attempt to establish that morality is an extension of self-love, either in the form of a developed egoism, or in the form of self-love transposed into love of the other in sympathy. The attempt to demonstrate this unity conceals from the theorist the fact that self-interest and morality represent two distinct levels of individual life, and that they must be related so as to subordinate self-interest to the claims of morality. Once it becomes apparent that the attempt to identify the two is unsatisfactory, the distinction between them and hierarchical ordering of them is clearly understood, but their harmonization and the motivational power of morality becomes incomprehensible.

That rationalism is the implicit truth of the earlier theories can be seen in the following way: these latter theories seek to show how, from an initial position of subjective individualism, the altruistic principle of equality can be made intelligible.

My claim has been that any attempt to show the connection between that initial position and altruism implicitly assumes in its account of the initial position the principle of altruism itself. In other words, what purports to be a subjective egoism is, in effect, objective egoism. Consequently, one cannot explain the motivational force of the altruist principle because of its necessary connexion with self-interested motivational forces. Its motivational force must, therefore, stand on its own.

Subjective egoism is the position according to which the individual is an end for himself, but only a subjective end. As I have argued above (together with others) this attitude of the individual is perfectly compatible with his recognizing the reality of others as also subjectively ends for themselves. Given the coherence of this, there is no conceivable way in which one can move from here to the altruist principle. Altruism involves a completely new principle. It can only be derived from the initial position if it is already contained in it. This implicit use of the altruist principle is present in those formulations which I have called objective egoism, according to which the individual is an end for himself, but treats himself implicitly as an objective end. This conception of himself as an objective end must be analysed into a subjective element, the individual's actual choice of particular values, and an objective element, the principle that beings who are self-formers, or free agents, are of objective value. This is, of course, already the altruist principle. It is disguised in the objective egoist because he claims to be the only being to which the principle applies. It is not difficult to show that he is inconsistent in claiming this. Thus he must accept the full altruist principles applicable to any agent whatsoever.

Arguments such as Gewirth's, discussed earlier, clearly involve this implicit use of the altruist principle in the initial position. This is true also of the universalizability principle. These are, however, already rationalist type arguments, and I need to show that the sympathy and egoistic theories of morality depend upon the same implicit assumption. In the case of sympathy, this has already been done. Let me briefly recall the argument. In the sympathy theory altruism is the result of seeing oneself in the other, and feeling for him as one feels for oneself. But this could only produce the altruist principle if it involved the transfer to the other of claims that one makes for oneself, and these claims must be of an objective egoistic nature. Recognizing the other as like oneself is seeing that the objective value that one claims for oneself applies equally to him. But if one's initial claim is that of the objective egoist, then it is not a special sentiment that is necessary to make one love the other as oneself, for one is implicitly committed to a principle which makes it rationally necessary for one to value others equally with oneself.

Egoism in its Hobbesian form may appear not to be of an objective nature. But in so far as it is not, it is obviously unsatisfactory and cannot succeed in showing how a commitment to the equal liberty principle is in each individual's self-interest. However, Hobbesian-type egoism often involves an equivocation as to whether an individual's self-interest is to be defined in terms of an original subjective egoist standpoint, in which case the argument breaks down, or whether it is to be defined in terms of the common interest individuals have in the principle of equal liberty. Since the equal liberty principle is essentially an affirmation of the equal value of agents as such, if this is understood as in itself each individual's self-interest, it must mean that each individual's egoistic interest is to be treated as in itself an objective value. But this is objective egoism, and the argument would be that the condition of objective egoism is the equal liberty principle. While this pretends to reduce morality to self-interest, in fact it implicitly assumes the altruist principle within the definition of self-interest.

UTILITARIANISM

The argument so far to the effect that modern individualist ethical thought produces a radical separation and opposition between the particular and moral dimensions of individual and social life, as a consequence of the ever-present potential for conflict between values, has ignored the possibility of interpreting the fundamental principle of altruism in a way which will produce subordinate principles capable of determining objectively the relative claims of individuals arising from such conflicts. Alternatively, the principle of utility might be brought in as an independent but secondary principle for resolving them. Since utilitarianism can be treated as a modern ethical theory standing on its own and as a rival to the theories that I have so far been discussing, I must now say something about how utilitarianism relates to these theories, before going on to discuss the possibility of objective subordinate ordering principles.

Utilitarianism in its classical form affirms that what is objectively good is happiness understood as a sum of pleasures. The principle of utility can be formulated without specifying what it is that has supreme value, but in that case one is interested only in the *form* of utilitarian arguments, namely their consequentialist structure. My concern, however, is with substantive ethical doctrines, and so with utilitarianism in so far as it is committed to a specific view as to the nature of the supreme value in ethics. The dominant utilitarian view of this is that it consists in happiness.

If happiness is the good, the rights of persons will be derived from the supreme principle by considering what social arrangements will maximize happiness. In this form utilitarianism is a clear alternative to the view hitherto discussed which sees the ground of value to consist in individuals as self-forming beings. Let us begin with the Benthamite understanding of happiness: for him the fundamental ground of value in utilitarian theory is pleasure and the avoidance of pain.[90] Because this is fundamental, it is claimed that it is underivable from anything else, and hence not amenable to an ultimate proof.[91] Since, on this view, the source of the good does not lie in human beings specifically, pleasure must be accorded a value wherever it occurs, in all sentient beings whatever. If men are to count more than animals, it can be only because men, being capable of greater

---

[90] J. Bentham, *Introduction to the Principles of Morals and Legislation*, Basil Blackwell, 1948, p. 125.
[91] ibid., p. 128.

sentience, are potentially more productive of pleasure and pain. If a purely quantitative notion of pleasure is maintained, we can claim that a human being dissatisfied is better than a pig satisfied only by virtue of the greater potential satisfactions locked up in the human pleasure producing machine.

Utilitarianism is often derided as a pig philosophy, one in which the human being has worth only as a more complex pig. But, as J. S. Mill points out, this ignores the fact that, while pleasure is the good, individuals are not required by the theory to seek as much pleasure for themselves as possible, but to pursue disinterestedly the greatest amount of pleasure altogether.[92] It involves altruistic action as disinterestedly neutral between one individual and another, including the agent himself, just as much as the theory that attributes worth to man as such. Utilitarianism is, therefore, a moral theory, but it produces just the same division between the individual as particular being seeking his own pleasure, and the individual as pure moral agent seeking the general pleasure, as the theory hitherto discussed. On the one hand, the individual is the complex pig, but on the other he is the pure moral agent.[93]

As disinterested moral agents men must treat each other, in respect of their potential for producing pleasure and pain, as of equal value. But this is merely to say that one man's unit of pleasure is to count equally with any other man's, or in other words units of pleasure have equal value in whomsoever they occur. This is not to treat the human individual as having any value other than as that in which pleasure occurs, as one might treat the value of a plot of land in terms of its potential for producing what one really values, for example wheat.

[92] J. S. Mill, *Utilitarianism*, J. M. Dent, 1944, pp. 10 and 16.
[93] Utilitarianism thus does not escape the problem of explaining how morality is possible. One finds in utilitarian writers versions of the objective egoist argument (see Mackie, op. cit., pp. 142–3) and also of the sympathy and benevolence theories. I shall not concern myself with these issues in respect of utilitarian theory, or indeed with many other issues arising from it. My purpose in this section is limited to showing the unsatisfactoriness of utilitarian theory in so far as it entirely rejects individualist value theory, and the impossibility of achieving a synthesis between them.

The utilitarian principle is, then, a simple aggregative one implying nothing about how pleasures ought to be distributed between men. No man as such has a claim to have any pleasure at all, but only to have his pleasures and pains counted in the determination of that arrangement which will produce a greater surplus of pleasure over pain than any alternative. However, if we add empirical assumptions about men we can get a result that may look in practice much more like the ethical theory that grounds value in individuals. Thus, if we say that each man is the best judge of his own interests, or of what gives him pleasure, then a social arrangement in which men have the freedom to express their interests will be a condition of maximizing happiness. This would be an equal freedom, since we would have empirical grounds for holding that *each* man judges his own interests better than others judge them for him. The pure moral agent will have to follow individuals' own accounts of themselves in the first place, but he still has to determine what distribution of resources to individuals, by which each can move towards the realization of his pleasure potential, will produce the greatest amount of happiness altogether. Individuals are still valuable simply as potential for producing units of pleasure, but they have this peculiarity that each machine alone knows its own workings, and so must be consulted concerning it.

Thus while this empirically based claim to freedom involves an equal freedom, since each alone knows how he works, it does not involve an equal right to the means of happiness, since the freedom is just a condition of the moral agent's knowledge of the machinery for maximizing happiness. An argument for equality can be produced, if we make further empirical assumptions about the diminishing marginal utility of pleasure-giving resources. If the marginal utility of resources to each man rises and declines in the same way, then an equal distribution of the means of happiness will be required, assuming that there are no costs involved in re-distributing resources and no side-effects on the production of resources. However, quite apart from the uncertainty of these empirical claims, it is to be noted that the activity of the moral agent involves the assumption that all the means to happiness are available for it to distribute in accordance with the moral principle. This is a peculiar assumption and will be considered shortly in the discussion of subordinate ordering principles.

The empirical assumptions, which justify freedom and equality as instrumental values, do not alter the basic characteristic of the theory that it treats man simply as an instrument for producing or recording pleasure. The emphasis on pleasure results in Smart's problem as to whether, if we had invented a way of stimulating the pleasure centres of our brain through plugging electrodes into it, and if operating electrodes produced more pleasure than any alternative, we would want to say that this is the best life for man.[94] Perhaps this question arises for the individualist also; for what if the individual chooses to spend a life as an electrode operator? However, in so far as the individualist theory holds that value resides in the individual as a self-forming being, it is incompatible with the *choice* of a purely passive existence, for this is a case, like choosing to be a slave, in which one freely chooses to give up one's self-forming activity. It would be an inauthentic life.

The unattractiveness and unacceptability of the utilitarian theory in its classic Benthamite form consists in its denial that any value resides in the individual as a self-forming being. This denial follows from its understanding of happiness as a sum of pleasures: in consequence men can be distinguished from the animals, and higher from lower pleasures, only in terms of their greater fecundity in respect of pleasure. It might be thought possible to alter this conception of happiness, while preserving the general utilitarian claim that happiness is the supreme value.

In trying to make more acceptable the notion of happiness as the supreme value, we would want to say that the pleasure involved in the pursuit of essentially human activities, e.g. intellectual activity, artistic activity, but more generally any

---

[94] J. J. C. Smart and B. Williams, *Utilitarianism For and Against*, Cambridge University Press, p. 18.

activity which involves performing in accordance with a consciously set standard, is not the same kind of state of being as that involved in the immediate physical pleasures of the animal organism. The former kind of pleasure arises in beings who have consciously set themselves ends of action, and the pleasure results from the attainment of the ends and the progress towards their attainment. The so-called lower and physical pleasures of the human organism are also transformed in man by becoming part of the complex consciously set ends of men. The values attached to them cease to be purely physical ones.

Let us still call this satisfaction of desire happiness. Happiness for men consists in the satisfaction resulting from their attainment of their main ends in life, or from their being on the way to such attainment. Happiness is still the good, but we have now built into the concept of happiness a distinctively human component. The good for man is not simply the satisfaction of desire, but the satisfaction of *human* desire, and is qualitatively distinct from the good for animals. However, we have begun to construct a notion of the good for man which includes a conception of him as a self-forming being. Only in so far as he forms himself by setting himself ends to realize in his life can he achieve that good which consists in the attainment of self-determined ends. But why should we treat the satisfaction as alone the good? Since the satisfaction is only an element in a whole process in which individuals form themselves, the good must include that process. We cannot understand the good for man apart from the good of human freedom. Freedom, or self-determination, is not a means to the end of satisfaction of desire, but an integral part of what it is for a man to be happy.

By moving along this line of argument, we are retracing our steps to the notion that men have worth in respect of their individuality, or self-determining nature, and in the process we lose the specifically utilitarian character of the ethical theory. This is, indeed, the direction J. S. Mill took in his attempt to modify the Benthamite doctrine without abandoning it. The result is, nevertheless, a confusion. This can be seen in the first place in the famous qualitative distinction Mill makes between higher and lower pleasures. This is intended to justify the superiority of an unsatisfied man to a satisfied pig, and an unsatisfied Socrates to a satisfied fool.[95] This could be a distinction between the potential in different organisms for carrying on activities that are more fecund in pleasures, and thus produce a greater quantity of pleasure than lower activities. But if we interpret the distinction in Mill to mean that the higher intellectual pleasures are *not* higher because the activities which produce them are quantitatively more productive, then it must be in virtue of something other than pleasure that the higher pleasures deserve their exalted status. Hence the highest good is not pleasure. Of course, Mill does not tell us what the highest good is, for he wishes to combine utilitarianism with anti-quantitative notions of pleasure. But since the higher pleasures are defined in terms of mind, and since the point of the distinction is to justify the unsatisfied intelligence in Socrates or man relative to the satisfied fool or pig, it is obvious enough that Mill is implicitly conceiving, as the source of higher value, the capacity of men to think about their lives and choose a life for themselves, in which course they can well remain unsatisfied in a way that the unthinking pig or human fool cannot.

In the second place there is the value Mill places on individuality, or a self-determined life, in *On Liberty*. The basic theme of the work is that individuality is the condition of well being for men. Happiness involves the realization of ends which men themselves have chosen. Hence the fundamental value is not the satisfaction of desire as such, but the realization of self-chosen ends, which incorporates in it the notion of the value of the individual as a self-forming being. This is, indeed, what Mill says: individuality is not a means to happiness, but an integral part of the end.[96] To this extent, then, Mill has abandoned the utilitarian position. But he wishes to deny that he has, and seeks to preserve the utilitarian framework for his valuation of individuality, by claiming that the rights to liberty that he is affirming are not natural rights, or the inherent rights

95 J. S. Mill, op. cit., p. 9.
96 J. S. Mill, *On Liberty*, J. M. Dent, 1944, p. 115.

of men, but are derived from utility, the utility of man as a progressive being. By this he means man's capacity to produce higher forms of life, and so higher pleasures. Liberty is required as a necessary means to develop these new forms of life. This formulation trades on the ambiguity in the concept of higher pleasures. If this is the qualitative distinction discussed above, the utilitarianism of it is only apparent. Furthermore, the argument appears to demote liberty from being an integral part of the end, to being once more only a means. But he has already described liberty as part of the end, and so clearly desires to have the argument both ways.

In the essay on *Utilitarianism* Mill attempts explicitly to reconcile the Benthamite position on the nature of the ultimate value in ethics with the individualist theory as it is expressed in the idea of the priority of justice over utility. Mill seeks to show that justice is, as utilitarians must claim, a secondary and derivative principle, but that it is of such peculiar importance, because of its close connexion with the fundamental condition of human happiness, namely security, that individualists may be forgiven for thinking that it is an independent principle in its own right. Justice involves for Mill an equality of right, in the first instance the right not to be harmed by others. It is in the understanding of this equality that we find Mill's greatest confusion. In order to preserve the fundamentals of the utilitarian position, equality must be understood, as I have indicated above, as the equal value to be accorded to equal units of pleasure wherever such units are to be found, and claims to an equal distribution of resources must depend on empirical assumptions about the diminishing marginal utility of resources to men. But Mill wants to say that utilitarianism involves an equal right to happiness, which includes an equal right to the means of happiness. According to the Benthamite view there could be no such thing as an equal right to happiness, if this means that each man has as good a claim to be happy and so to the means of his happiness as any other man. For no one has any claim other than to have his units of pleasure and pain counted in the calculation of the total. Given the relevant empirical assumptions a right to an equal amount of resources can be derived, but it is not derived from a right of the individual to his happiness; whereas Mills affirms the equal right as following *directly* from the utilitarian principle itself. Equality in a significant sense, the equal value of men, is built into the utilitarian principle.[97] Here, then, is the most complete confusion between the utilitarian principle on the one hand, and the individualist theory, which attributes value to individuals as such, on the other. If the utilitarian principle affirms that pleasure alone is the good, it cannot also be the case that the value of individuals as such is part of that principle.

The argument about the status of the rules of justice and the principle of equality relative to the principle of utility is a form of the debate between act- and rule-utilitarians. A rule-utilitarian holds that we do not have to apply the utilitarian principle directly to possible acts in order to determine the right action in each circumstance, but only to general rules under which possible particular acts fall. Thus having determined the utility of a general rule, e.g. the practice of promising, we do not have to consider the utility of each act that falls under the practice, but must perform it because of the utility of the practice in general. If overruling by other considerations is to be accepted, it must be by the application of other utilitarianly good rules which produce requirements in the particular case which conflict with the requirement to keep one's promise. Thus one might want to say that the equal rights involved in the notion of justice was a practice which was utilitarianly good, not because equality was part of the meaning of utility, but because it was a means to it. The question is, however, whether this makes sense. Whether it does or not depends on what one takes to be involved in the nature of the practice of justice. If we mean by the principle of justice, the basic rule requiring that persons be given an equal value, then we are involved in the absurdity of on the one hand affirming a principle of equal value which commits us to valuing individuals in themselves, and on the other hand claiming that the

[97] J. S. Mill, *Utilitarianism*, p. 58.

value of this principle lies in its relation to another principle which holds that pleasure alone is the good. Justice, as a binding rule involving the principle of equal value, cannot coherently be said to be utilitarianly good.

Recognizing the equality principle as a fundamental one involves abandoning utilitarianism understood as *the valid* ethical theory. But could one combine the individualist theory with the utility principle by holding that the latter serves as a secondary principle for resolving conflicts that arise from the operation of the primary principle of equal value? The question would be whether the principle of utility as a subordinate ordering principle would be compatible with the primary principle. This is not the case. If the primary principle affirms the equal value of individuals, then a necessary condition of a satisfactory secondary principle is that it orders the conflicts arising from the operation of the primary principle in such a way as not to infringe that principle itself. The secondary principles must preserve the equality of men, by not discriminating in favour of one rival claimant or the other. It does not seem that utilitarianism as a secondary principle can preserve that neutrality.

SUBORDINATE ORDERING PRINCIPLES

Any principle that can be used to resolve the conflicts that arise between the authentic particular choices of individuals would have to preserve the equality of the conflicting agents; otherwise they could not be mutually acceptable. There must also be a uniquely valid set of such principles, or, alternatively, valid but different principles must have the same distributive effects in order to ensure that the equality condition continues to be met. It is immediately obvious that the principles of this kind that we have, which claim to be derivations from the basic equal freedom of men, have very different distributive effects, and are largely espoused for this reason. If it cannot be shown that one of these sets is the uniquely valid one, but if on the contrary it turns out to be the case that each has a partial validity as an interpretation of the basic principle, then subordinate ordering principles cannot remove the incoherence of the basic principle. Indeed my claim will be that the possibility of justifying in terms of the basic principle quite opposed secondary principles, roughly classical liberal at one extreme and 'egalitarian'[98] at the other, is the consequence of the incoherence in the basic principle itself, the split that it contains between the particular and moral dimensions of individual and social life.

It should be noticed that even if it were possible to arrive at a uniquely valid set of subordinate ordering principles, the relation of the particular self to the moral self would be left unchanged. Despite the existence of objective determinations of an individual's particular rights, the conflict between these and an individual's authentic particular choices for his life would still leave the particular and moral levels of the individual in unreconciled opposition. There would certainly be an oddity about this result, since through objective conflict-ordering principles one would be able to order the oppositions between particular interests in a neutral way, and so in a way that no particular individual could complain of. But it is not the individual as a particular being who is satisfied with equality and seeks its more concrete determination, but the individual as moral being. Hence, however determinate and coherent a set of objective particular rights and duties may be arrived at, the particular self, because of the nature of its authentic self-determination, will continue to find itself in an ever-present potential opposition.

THE LIBERAL THEORY OF EQUAL FREEDOM

The major issue which the secondary principles seek to determine is how access to the resources necessary to develop and express one's conception of one's life is to be regulated. If resources were in unlimited supply relative to claims upon them, no conflict-ordering principles would be necessary. Further-

---

[98] This is not a very satisfactory term, but I mean by it a substantive rather than a formal equality.

more, however access is to be regulated, the principles must contain both an interpretation of freedom and an interpretation of equality. The liberal theory is not to be understood as simply choosing freedom and rejecting equality, and the egalitarian theory to be understood as doing the reverse; equality is essential to the liberal position and freedom to the egalitarian one.

By the classical liberal theory I mean the one to be found in Locke's *Second Treatise* and in much of nineteenth-century thought and vigorously re-affirmed today by Nozick and others. According to this view the entitlement of individuals to holdings, as Nozick calls them, arises from the individual's own independent activity. Individuals appropriate through their own effort and enterprise parts of the earth's resources, and acquire other resources, through whatever exchange relations they can establish with others. The entitlement of individuals is not determined by some moral and collective authority. We have what appears to be a contrast between a theory which holds that resources are first owned only through the activity of individuals, and one which holds that they are initially collectively owned and only subsequently distributed to individuals for use or consumption.

The liberal theory needs, then, a theory of acquisitions (how individuals acquire entitlements to holdings), a theory of transfers, together with a theory of the rectification of injustice.[99] The main problem is presented by the theory of acquisitions. Given an initial legitimate acquisition of holdings by individuals, transfers are to be understood as valid provided that they occur through the free disposal of his holding by the owner himself either through gift or contract, neither of which notions present any special difficulty. So how do individuals acquire holdings legitimately in the first place? The classic version of such an account is Locke's, which Nozick more or less follows: a just initial appropriation is one in which individuals through their own activity and for their own use appropriate previously unappropriated parts of nature. Our starting-point must be a world of untouched nature with only a few

[99] R. Nozick, *Anarchy, State and Utopia*, Basil Blackwell, 1974, p. 150.

individuals who begin the process of appropriation. As the number of individuals increases, more and more of the world gets appropriated, but provided present holdings are held through legitimate transfers which can be traced back to legitimate original appropriations, these current holdings are also valid.

The major difficulty in this account arises from appropriations which worsen other men's position. If one man appropriates the only water hole in an area, with the result that others will die of thirst, the appropriation cannot be valid. Hence, there must be a proviso on original appropriations which safeguards the claims of others. In Locke this consists in the requirement that 'enough and as good [be] left in common for others'.[100] Strictly interpreted this proviso must rule out the legitimacy of any appropriation that leaves others without any of the thing to appropriate for themselves, assuming that they wish to do so. Since, after the whole world has been appropriated, there is nothing left for latecomers to appropriate, the proviso would mean that the last appropriation which did not leave anything in common for others must have been illegitimate; and so on back to the first appropriation which made it impossible for subsequent appropriators to satisfy the proviso, and thus made them worse off than they would have been but for the initial appropriation.[101]

This effectively cancels the validity of all private appropriations once the world fills up with men. To avoid this conclusion Nozick proposes that the relevant interpretation of the Lockean proviso does not consist in the loss of opportunities to improve one's position by appropriation, but in the loss of the free use of resources that one had hitherto enjoyed. Latecomers who had never enjoyed the use would have no claim. Is it, then, intended that destitute latecomers in a fully appropriated world have no claim against resource-holders whatsoever? Here Nozick, as Locke before him, suggests that in a world of private appropriation, the amount of resources available for use by men will have

[100] J. Locke, *Two Treatises of Government*, Second Treatise, Section 27.
[101] R. Nozick, op. cit., pp. 175–6.

been so greatly increased through the increased productive powers of labour that all could be better off than they would have been in a state of the world in which parts of nature remained unappropriated for them to use freely. The difficulty with this argument, as Nozick makes clear,[102] is that of determining the original position or baseline in terms of which the position of latecomers can be assessed. The free use of nature would seem to exclude a primitive agricultural life, but would it exclude also the life of hunters and pastoralists, who permanently appropriate (although not individually no doubt) parts of nature? Perhaps the baseline should be determined by a hypothetical natural man's existence along the lines of Rousseau's conception of the original state of nature, in which natural man lives an individually isolated life, and whose level of existence is that of any other animal in nature.

In so far as the theory of acquisitions says that one is entitled to appropriate what does not belong to another within the limits of the Lockean proviso, it states merely a necessary condition of legitimate acquisition. It does not explain how it is possible to acquire a right in a thing that does not belong to another. Locke derives the right from the individual's prior ownership of his body, so that whatever one mixes one's labour with, or whatever is the product of one's labour, becomes one's property. Nozick somewhat half-heartedly follows Locke here, faute de mieux.[103] The notions of owning one's own body, owning the labour of one's body and the work of one's hands, that is to say having a right claim against others in respect of these things, themselves require explanation. How does one acquire a right in one's own body? Do animals have such a right? Presumably not if we can legitimately use them as beasts of burden. Is it the human capacity to exercise self-control, and so *take possession* of one's body that creates such a right? Of course, Locke at this point has recourse to God as his explanation. But leaving such a meta-human principle aside, it is obvious that the mere taking possession by the individual of his own powers, through developing his capacity of self-control

---

[102] ibid., p. 177. [103] ibid., pp. 174–5.

cannot establish an *objective* right. For this relation of the individual to his body and to what he can do with it can be understood subjectively: he makes this possession a value for him, but not a value for anyone. If there is an objective right of the individual in his own body and its products, it must be the result of the endorsement by a morally legislative will of such self-activity. *It* bestows the authority the individual has to exclude others from the use of his body and the appropriation of his body's products.

Such a morally authoritative will, however, presupposes that the world's resources are available for it to determine how access to them is to be legitimated. It assumes a prior right to ownership on its own part. It legislates to the effect that each self-possessing individual can appropriate what does not belong to another, provided he leaves enough and as good in common for others.[104] This produces the liberal conception of private property right, provided that we start with abundant resources in an original state of nature. Suppose that some refugees from a devastated area land on an uninhabited island, and that the resources are not sufficient for each to appropriate as much as he needs; since all arrive at the same time, the initial entitlement of each must be an equal one, each can have a right only to appropriate an equal share relative to his needs. In such a case the right to private property is determined not by the individual act of appropriation, but by the morally authoritative will which determines each man's share. It is through the individual act of taking possession of the thing that the right is embodied; but the right is not created by this pure individual activity. This is true, also, of an original state of nature with abundant resources. The individual act of taking possession does not create the right, but merely gives actuality to it.

The independence of individual rights to resources from a superior authoritative will cannot be, then, what is of central

[104] Kant recognizes that the right of private appropriation depends on the 'innate common possession of the earth's surface, and on the a priori general will corresponding to it, which permits private possession' (*Metaphysical Elements of Justice*, The Library of Liberal Arts, 1965, p. 57).

importance in liberal theory. This is clear even in Locke, since for him God is such a superior will. The main point consists firstly in the requirement to actualize that right through the individual activity of appropriation. Consequently, the theory legitimates the individual in doing whatever he likes with his validly acquired resources within the limits of the rights of others. The important consequence I wish to emphasize here is that as long as individuals transfer resources to each other through free contracts and gifts, and nobody is harmed, i.e. no third party is made worse off by such exchange, then whatever degree of inequality that results is just.

Nozick expresses this claim through the parable of Wilt Chamberlain.[105] Suppose an initial distribution of resources based on some idea of a correct pattern of holdings. Wilt Chamberlain has a scarce skill at basketball and is greatly in demand. He agrees to play for a team on terms that give him a certain proportion of the price of tickets. Spectators on buying their ticket have to place a separate sum into the W.C. box for each game that W.C. plays in. As he is greatly in demand, attendance is very high, and W.C.'s earnings are very large. Resources are freely and legitimately transferred in this way from many individuals to W.C. who can use them to fructify, and so acquire a greater share of a possibly expanding total. The liberal theory justifies this position.

The justification is that no one is made worse off through the transfers, and hence there is no way of overruling them without infringing the fundamental principle of the right to freedom to which both liberals and anti-liberal egalitarians adhere. This argument holds, even if we start with a preferred egalitarian distribution. But, then, from the liberal point of view it would not seem to matter what theory of acquisitions we have, since we can apply directly the fundamental right to freedom to justify the individual's right to enter into whatever exchange relations he pleases. As long as the initial distribution of resources is valid, then the right to freedom requires the right to exchange such resources freely, the results of which will be

[105] Nozick, op. cit., pp. 161–3.

validated by the initial distribution. Yet without an appropriate theory of acquisitions, the argument looks vulnerable. For the initial distribution, if valid, invalidates the inegalitarian conclusion, and we are left with an incoherence. An appropriate theory of acquisitions would eliminate this incoherence by denying the validity of the initial distribution. The initial allocation of resources is valid according to the liberal theory only as a consequence of the activity of individuals in appropriating unowned nature. Hence there would be no way of upsetting the resulting inequality, so long as the Lockean proviso is satisfied.

The liberal theory emphasizes the right of individuals to negative freedom, i.e. the right to do what they like without being interfered with by others. It is the right of the particular will to form and pursue its choices without external determination. The liberal theory affirms this as the *sole* valid principle for determining a legitimate distribution, and because of this private appropriation and transfer must be the sole means through which entitlements are established. Although the theory emphasizes the negative freedom of the individual it is still an equal freedom which is at issue, and because of this there necessarily lies behind the particular will, the moral will as its presupposition and ground. But if the moral will has a superior right to the particular will, the liberal theory as an account of the *sole* valid distributive principle cannot be correct.

EGALITARIANISM

The sole operation of the liberal principle ensures for empirical reasons that the distribution of resources between men will become very unequal. Thus some men will have greater means to attain their ends than others. Of course, in practice individuals to a considerable extent tailor their ends to fit their means, as a necessary strategy for survival in a world in which resources are not distributed in accordance with men's needs. But it is precisely such a world which can from a certain point of view appear morally unacceptable. From this point of view the sole valid distributive principle is that of needs. I understand by needs, here, not simply men's basic needs for health, shelter or even for a socially defined minimum standard of living, but their needs relative to the plan of life they have formed, the ideal content of their freedom.[106] Assuming that resources are not sufficient to meet everyone's needs to the full, the appropriate distribution would be one of proportionate equality. Everyone should receive resources sufficient to satisfy the same proportion of his needs. Perhaps we could distinguish in people's plans for their lives a main idea with subordinate elements, and hold that only the main idea counts as a need, the remainder being wants. Then we would aim to distribute resources until everyone's needs are fulfilled before using any surplus to satisfy wants in accordance with proportionate equality.[107] However the difficulties in elaborating a practical distributive principle on the basis of needs need not detain us, since my aim here is to exhibit the grounds for such a principle and its relation to the requirement of freedom.

The basic egalitarianism of this view consists in the idea not that each should have absolutely the same amount of resources, but that each man's plan of life is of equal worth, and that consequently he has as good a claim to the resources necessary to realize his plan as any other. The plans must be authentic ones: one cannot, for instance, include in one's plan a desire to be superior to others. For, then, one's end would be dependent on how one stood in relation to others, and would be in part determined by them rather than independently of them.

While this type of egalitarianism is nowhere practised (in respect of a whole society), and does not find too many adherents as the uniquely valid distributive principle, it is often taken as the valid starting-point for just distributive principles. Departures from an initially equal (or proportionately equal) distribution can be allowed provided everyone gains from the inequality.[108] As a starting-point it presumes that all resources

[106] See above p. 15 and D. Miller, op. cit., ch. 4.
[107] Miller, op cit., pp. 143–50.
[108] This is the position in G. Vlastos, op. cit., and of course in Rawls's *Theory of Justice*, in which form I will be considering it shortly.

are available for or owned by some agency to distribute in accordance with its own criteria of justice. The agency here is a moral one. It is the standpoint of the moral self according to which all particular selves have equal worth. How does this entitle the moral self to assume control over resources for particular selves? Since the worth of a particular self is determined only by the moral self, its entitlement to resources is so determined also, irrespective of whatever de facto appropriation has occurred. It is only the moral will that legitimizes possession of resources. As we have seen, this is true of the liberal position, which presupposes an initial common ownership and a general will authorizing private appropriation. It makes no difference to this basic claim of the moral self to determine a just distribution, whether some individuals have in fact acquired control over resources by their individual effort, skill, and enterprise, and so might be held to deserve them more than other individuals who live in poverty as a result of their incompetence or inactivity. From the point of view of the moral self the greater natural abilities of one man relative to another do not create any greater moral worth, and so a higher claim to have his ends realized.

The moral self has to acknowledge the right of the particular self to make substantive choices for its life having regard only to itself. For the moral self as an impersonal, non-particularized agent cannot make these choices itself, indeed any at all of a substantive nature. For it is only as the particular self forms itself by making its own choices that it has moral worth. However, the right of the particular to make such choices must be dissociated from its ability to acquire resources, and from its development of skills or capacities which are means to the realization of such choices. The moral self must see the assets available in the world for the realization of human purposes, including the skills of individuals, as in principle collective assets, the distribution of which it is for the moral self to determine. From this point of view individuals have no right to use their own capacities as they think fit for their private ends. As a collective asset of mankind they must be used to produce resources which will be available for distribution according to need. Men must continue to form for themselves their private projects, but such private willing must be divorced from the particular activity of individuals as producers of goods and services. Particular willing of this latter kind involving the active use of men's capacities must be identical with moral willing on the assumption that the moral will has complete control or possession of the means of particular willing, namely the capacities of individuals.

Such a system of particular willing would constitute a centrally directed economic society, although the central direction could be understood to operate through each individual's moral will, common to all, which directs the individual in the use of his particular abilities. The *particular* self could not, of course, make the required divorce between the two types of particular willing, or treat his particular abilities as a common asset to be used for the common good. It must see them as ways and means of realizing its plan of life. Indeed it is difficult to see how for the particular individual there can be any separation between plan of life and development of abilities, unless plans of life are purely plans for consumption. This may involve the development of capacities for appreciation, for distinguishing good and bad products, but the talents involved would be those of a passive and leisured life, not the active ones associated with the development of one's productive powers in industry or art. That consumption must be an element in men's private ends is certain, but according to this view consumption will be the only content, and all production will be collective.

Perhaps the individual will see his private end in producing for the common good, and in developing his talents for all to benefit? But, in the first place, the individual's private ends must be authentic; hence if he is going to pursue the benefit of all, it must be as his particular plan for his life, and there is no reason to suppose that particular plans will have such a content. Secondly, even if they were all to include general benevolence, this could not be the same as an impersonal benevolence without destroying the basis of private desire on which benevolence can operate. As part of the plans of individuals for their lives, private benevolence must be arbitrary from a moral point of view. Whether it coincides with the dictates of impersonal benevolence or not must be a contingent matter. However much private benevolence exists, there is still likely to be a conflict between particular wills and moral will and hence a rejection by the particular will of the moral will's claims on its abilities. Obviously a condition of the coherence of a particular self is the integration of its abilities with its ends; so their separation in the above way is unsatisfactory. What would be needed to resolve this difficulty is a situation in which the content of each individual's plan of life coincided with the production of resources by himself that he wished others to benefit from in accordance with the requirements of impersonal benevolence, that is to say a harmony of particular and moral wills. But this is always the condition for resolving the moral problem. Where the particular and moral wills are identified in abstraction and separation from each other, their content can only coincide by chance.

Just as the liberal theory has a totally implausible view of how individuals acquire entitlement to resources, so does the egalitarian theory have a totally implausible view of the ownership of human assets located in individuals' bodies.

It is obvious that the consequence of the legislation of the moral self for an equal distribution of the means to the attainment of one's ends is an infringement of the rights of the particular self to its freedom. The rule of equality requires that no one be able to acquire through his own enterprise and virtue a superior position to any other, even if such individual enterprise is the result of transactions which make no-one worse off. But it is irrational for the moral self to forbid transactions which make some people better off and none worse off. This defines a Pareto-optimal position, and it is widely considered irrational not to be in such a position.[109] Pareto-optimality may be attacked on the grounds that it refers to the rights of the particular self to secure the best position for itself, so long as it

[109] See on this J. Rawls, op. cit., p. 66 f.

does not infringe certain moral restraints, and it may then be argued that the definition of these restraints must have priority over what is permitted to the particular self. If a move to a Pareto-optimal position infringes some definition of moral restraints, e.g. the egalitarian requirement itself, then in terms of that criterion the Pareto-optimal position is illegitimate. It carries no rational weight, and is of no importance if not met. But this merely begs the question as to the legitimacy of the Pareto criterion. Of course, in terms of the egalitarian principle a Pareto-optimal position, which infringes it, is illegitimate. But the problem arises because the primary principle, of which the above egalitarianism is an interpretation, involves the right of particulars to make choices for their lives having regard only to their own lives, the right of private will. The right of the particular will to its freedom must include the right to make any choices for itself which make it better off so long as it does not make anyone else worse off. If the egalitarian principle requires the rejection of this right, it undermines itself, since the above right is a corollary of the primary principle from which the egalitarian principle is derived.

The only way this result might be avoided is by the re-definition of what is involved in making another worse off. The individual's shifting relative position, not his absolute starting-point, would determine whether another had harmed him or not. This would ensure that one individual's gain in resources which left the absolute position of others unchanged would make them relatively worse off, and so count as harming them. But to make sense of this situation, it would have to be the case that the individual allows the value of his life to be determined, not by himself alone in accordance with the requirements of authentic choice, but from an external stand-point. The individual's purpose would consist in his having superior, or not having inferior, control of resources to others as evaluated according to some standard. This means that the individual is valuing his life as it would be valued by someone who valued a collection of individuals solely in accordance with their relative position in a whole order. The value of his life is not, therefore, ultimately value for himself, and thus something which he determines by and for himself alone, but is something determined from a standpoint external to him. In so far as the individual, in respect of his particular life, values himself ultimately from this standpoint, he values himself inauthentically.[110]

Thus whether we re-interpret the no-harm principle to cover the relative standing of individuals or not, the egalitarian interpretation of the primary principle is incompatible with the specification of the primary principle itself. As we have seen, the classical liberal interpretation also produces results which are incompatible with the inherently equal worth of men as choosers seen from the moral point of view. The liberal and egalitarian secondary principles are attempts to derive effective distributive principles from one-sided interpretations of the primary principle. That principle affirms the equal worth of men as self-forming beings, and hence requires a right of the particular self to form itself independently of others, a right to negative freedom, but at the same time involves the right of the moral self to pursue the welfare of each in an egalitarian way. The liberal and egalitarian theories concentrate on the right of the particular self and the right of the moral self respectively, and attempt to elaborate coherent principles in terms of the one right. But since they cannot exclude the other side of the principle without absurdity, they must conflict with the requirement of that side, and so fall into incoherence. It is for this reason that the claims of freedom (the right of the particular self) and the claims of equality (the right of the moral self) are popularly thought to be opposed to each other.

It might be thought that the incoherence in the secondary principles stems from the attempt to develop distributive principles in a one-sided way, and that what is needed is a way of combining them. But the attractions of one-sidedness here spring from the way in which the two elements in the primary principle are abstractly and separately identified. Given the in-

[110] Rousseau's account of human corruption in Part II of the *Discourse on Inequality* should be read in this way. See above pp. 59–62.

herent tendency for these elements to conflict, the possibility of coherence in distributive principles depends on the possibility of basing them on one side only. This cannot succeed. But the attempt to combine the two in a comprehensive theory of justice cannot succeed either, and as in the case of Rawls's theory, now to be considered, only multiplies confusion.

THE RAWLSIAN COMBINATION

The essential idea of this theory is that we start with the egalitarian position as an initially just baseline, but that we permit departures from an equal distribution provided that such inequalities serve to increase the total amount of resources available and hence make it possible for each to be better off than in the egalitarian position. Rawls has a particular version of the criterion for the permissible inequalities, or rather he specifies the criterion more exactly in the difference principle, which permits only those inequalities which maximize the long-run position of the least advantaged group in society. Thus we combine the egalitarian principle, that resources constitute a common pool to be distributed equally, which carries the implication that private self-seeking in respect of the production of resources is illegitimate, with the liberal principle which treats resources as inherently tied to private self-seekers, since we permit private self-seeking as a means of increasing the size of the common pool. This combination looks incoherent at first sight, and remains incoherent on further consideration.

The way in which Rawls seeks to deduce this combination of principles is through the idea of a contract in which self-interested persons choose principles of justice. They are supposed to choose firstly the egalitarian principle, in effect that primary social goods (by which he means liberty, opportunity, income and wealth and self-respect), be distributed equally.[111] The interesting point of this deduction is that the egalitarian principle, which I have claimed above expresses the interests of the moral self, is here presented as expressing the interests of

[111] Rawls, op. cit., p. 62.

the particular self. The plausibility of this deduction is essential to the apparent coherence of Rawls's overall position. For it makes the reversion to the normal expression of the interests of the particular self seem quite natural. Both the egalitarian and liberal elements are derived from the same principle, the rational choice of self-interested man.

These men choose in an original position which Rawls admits that he has designed specifically in order to produce results that conform to our moral intuitions.[112] The fundamental moral intuition that governs his conception of the original position is that it is morally wrong that individuals should gain advantage from their superior natural talents or social conditions, or suffer disadvantage from inferiority of talent or conditions.[113] This *is* the egalitarian principle. The liberal theory justifies the gains accruing to superior natural abilities, while it is the egalitarian principle that insists on the equal right of men to the means to realize their ends (primary social goods) whatever their natural talents.

How, then, does he design the original position so as to produce the egalitarian principle as the rational choice of self-interested men? In the first place the way in which the question of principles of justice is presented in the original position determines a certain kind of answer. The question is: how are the advantages of social cooperation to be distributed?[114] It is not the question to be found in earlier contract theories, viz. Hobbes's or Rousseau's how is social cooperation possible? On the contrary Rawls's question assumes that social cooperation is flourishing and the only problem for self-interested men is how to divide its gains among them.

The gains from social cooperation are the primary social goods, liberty, opportunity etc. In this list Rawls treats rights to liberty as goods of the same kind as income and wealth and to be distributed equally with these latter in the first instance. But if we start with self-interested individuals considering

---

[112] ibid., pp. 18 and 141.
[113] ibid., p. 15. See on this R. Nozick, op. cit., pp. 213–16.
[114] Rawls, op. cit., p. 4.

principles of justice, rights to liberty are not among the gains of social cooperation, but the necessary condition of it. This gives the principle of equal liberty an altogether different status from the one it holds in Rawls's theory, and ensures a primary validity for the liberal version. Since Rawls desires to give primary validity to the egalitarian principle, it is necessary for him to treat the right to liberty in this confused way. It enables him to pursue the issue as though it were not fundamentally one of how social cooperation is possible.

Yet this must be the basic question for him since he starts with self-interested men in an original position. It is simply and straightforwardly incoherent to suppose on the one hand that we are concerned with solely self-interested men and on the other that it is only the distribution of the gains from social cooperation and not social cooperation itself that is in question. The latter presupposes that men can already cooperate, while the former puts this at issue. Rawls's method of dealing with this is to say that he is not assuming human beings to be purely self-interested in the manner of Hobbes. They are assumed to be self-interested only in respect of the original position. Once the veil of ignorance is removed and men find themselves once more in actual social relations, they are perfectly capable of showing an interest in each other's interests, and so are perfectly capable of social cooperation. This is a fine example of having the argument both ways!

Let us ignore the absurdity of assuming purely self-interested men debating the division of gains from social cooperation, and consider how in this way Rawls purports to arrive at the general principle that social primary goods should be distributed equally unless an unequal division would make everyone better off. If we believe that men contribute unequally to the productivity of social cooperation and that individuals know their own contribution, this principle could not possibly be agreed to. To produce the desired result, then, Rawls assumes that his self-interested men are choosing principles of justice from behind a veil of ignorance as to their particular abilities, position, interests and ends in actual society. They know only the general facts about man and society, and so must choose principles which will protect their interests irrespective of what sort of person they turn out to be once the veil of ignorance is lifted. They must choose as though they were anyone. Rawls argues that in those conditions men will rationally choose the above general principle. This is the policy of maximizing the minimum, or making sure that the position of the worst off person in the division of advantages is as high as it could be. This obviously requires an equal distribution in the first instance. But an unequal distribution making everyone better off would be irrational for self-interested men to reject. More specifically inequalities which maximized the long-run position of the worst-off person would fulfil the requirements of maximizing the minimum. In fact Rawls's deduction of the maximin policy is generally considered unconvincing,[115] but I assume here that it is valid. The point is that by the veil of ignorance assumption Rawls makes the standpoint of the self-interested individual in some ways identical with the standpoint of the moral self. This is evident in the initial choice of an egalitarian distribution. More specifically, the attitude of the moral self is that resources constitute a common asset to be distributed so as to benefit each man equally. The veil of ignorance (plus the assumption of social cooperation) produces this result for self-interested men, because it makes them see resources as a common pool to be distributed in accordance with the interests of any man.

There is, however, a difference between the pure moral standpoint and that of self-interested men behind a veil of ignorance. The former requires that the productive activity of individuals should be directed towards producing resources for all to benefit from. It cannot admit the self-interest of producers. If producers are self-interested, then the level of production will depend on the incentive payments to individuals, and the attainment of maximum production will, given relevant natural

[115] See for instance B. Barry, *The Liberal Theory of Justice*, Clarendon Press, 1973, ch. 9, and R. M. Hare, 'Rawls's Theory of Justice' in N. Daniels (ed.), *Reading Rawls*, Basil Blackwell, 1975, pp. 102-7.

inequalities, require an unequal distribution of primary social goods. Here the assumption of self-interested men comes to the rescue. This evidently makes the self-interest of producers acceptable, so that if a larger total of resources which make everyone better off can be produced through unequal payments to producers, it will (roughly) be in every man's self-interest to approve such distributions. In this way we have combined both the egalitarian principle of the moral standpoint and the self-interested productive activity of the standpoint of the particular self, as contained in the liberal theory, and combined in an ordered relation to each other. The relevant claims of each are clearly specified (assuming the elaboration of the difference principle).

This result is arrived at through the assumption of social cooperation, which is illegitimate, but also through the assumption of the veil of ignorance. What is the justification for making this assumption? Rawls says that he does so in order to get the desired solution, and this means the solution that conforms to the moral standpoint. 'If the original position is to yield agreements that are just, the parties must be fairly situated and treated equally as moral persons.'[116] But, if the original position is designed so as to produce the desired moral standpoint, what weight does it add to that view? It appears to add weight because it appears to be an additional argument concerning self-interested rationality. Why does he not start with the moral standpoint immediately? Firstly, because a deduction of the moral standpoint is for obvious reasons desirable. But, secondly, his aim is to produce a theory of justice which combines the opposed liberal and egalitarian ones in an ordered whole, and, to achieve this, he cannot start with the moral standpoint, since he needs to incorporate the right of the particular self in production. None of this justifies the use of the veil of ignorance assumption. It is an *ad hoc* device to establish an identity of self-interest and morality. Why should individuals choosing principles behind a veil of ignorance in their own interest be committed to those principles, when the veil is

[116] Rawls, op. cit., p. 141.

removed, and they see that other principles would improve their position? Rawls cannot say, like Hobbes for example, that the human condition is *really* such that each man's self-interest lies in sticking by the equal liberty principle, for the Rawlsian men's self-interest in the principles of justice does not express what is really the case, but only what is the case behind a veil of ignorance. Thus when the individual is back in the actual world, the self-interest assumption is dropped.

In general my claim is that Rawls's theory is an attempt to establish allocative or distributive principles of justice based on the primary principle of the equal value of men as self-forming beings,[117] which combines elements from the liberal and egalitarian theories of justice. Thus it must combine the right of the particular self to negative freedom and the right of the moral self to pursue the welfare of each. It tries to do this by limiting the right of the particular self to negative freedom, as regards its access to resources, to only those arrangements which satisfy the difference principle, while this principle is determined by requirements in which the interests of the moral self in equality are primary. But, because it limits the right of the particular self within the difference principle, it must prohibit private activities which would be Pareto-optimal, in making some better off, and no-one worse off, which do not improve the position of the least advantaged group in society. And this as we have seen, is contrary to the requirements of the primary principle itself. The equal value of men as self-forming beings must involve the right to form one's life as one thinks fit provided one does not harm another. If this right does not exist, men cannot have equal value as self-forming beings. At the same time Rawls's theory, by allowing departures from equality, offends against the requirements of the moral self by giving some a greater opportunity to realize their ends than others, and hence denying their equal worth.

---

[117] I do not argue for this because it seems to me to be the obvious moral assumption of Rawls's work. Dworkin, however, shows this at some length. R. Dworkin, 'The Original Position', in N. Daniels (ed.), *Reading Rawls*.

The Rawlsian Combination

This criticism may be thought to be beside the point, for Rawls, in attempting to combine both the rights of the particular and moral self in an ordered relation, is committed to not treating the rights as absolutely valid, and hence is committed to limiting them by each other. The point in my criticism, however, is that in basing these rights on the individualist position, according to which the individual has value in himself, Rawls cannot avoid the consequences of that position. Because in the individualist theory the value of each is established independently of a relation to others, the right of the particular self requires the liberal theory, while the right of the moral self requires the egalitarian theory. A combination cannot be one which really makes them limit each other, but must show how *both* rights can be fully satisfied at the same time. This is the requirement that the claims of self-interest and those of morality harmonize through and through. In this respect the older individualists whom I have considered, Hobbes, Rousseau and Kant saw more clearly, but not ultimately more successfully, than contemporary ones.

Yet one might equally say that Rawls sees more clearly than the older individualists that a satisfactory conception of justice requires a mutual limitation of the rights to negative freedom and to welfare. But, finally, this cannot be done within an individualist conception of value.

Part II

In this section I consider the main lines of the ethical thought of two major theorists who are profoundly critical of individualist morality. The individualists fail to integrate the particular and general dimensions of individual life. Hegel and Marx are concerned specifically to overcome this alienation by re-integrating the particular with the general. My aim is to show that the overcoming of alienation in their theories involves so great an integration of particular with general that particular individuality is altogether absorbed in and destroyed by the general. This has to be demonstrated in the face of the theorists' own claims; for both see particular individuality not as opposed to the realization of the general, but as developed only along with with it.

HEGEL

According to the individualist theory, the individual has objective value in himself or is of absolute worth as such, and hence his particular life as chosen by him necessarily embodies this value. At the same time, since it is in respect of his nature as a man, which he shares with all other men, that the individual is of absolute worth, it must be true that the particular life of one individual cannot both embody absolute value and invade the particular life of another individual. So one must say that the particular will has worth only insofar as it respects the equal value of others. But since the particular will on the individualist view has value as an *immediate* embodiment of the single individual's absolute value, that is to say as it exists on its own, it cannot as a particular will be concerned with anything other than its own life and interest, certainly not with realizing the absolute value that lies in other individuals. The consequence is that the individualist conception of the immediate embodiment of absolute value in the single individual leads to a separation and opposition between the particular and universal (or absolute) dimension of individual life.

As we saw in Part 1 this self-division becomes explicit in Kantian rationalism, in the recognition that if moral value is to be realized and freedom is to be possible, pure reason, in virtue of which the individual is of absolute value, must itself be practical, or in other words must be capable of determining the particular will in accordance with substantive laws that are the product of itself, and hence purely rational. Kant failed to show, however, how substantive moral laws are deductions of pure reason with the result that in his thought pure reason (and the absolutely free will) remains an empty and unknown postulate of practical empirical life, neither integrated with it nor capable of determining it. It is true that Kant saw what had to be the case if the consequent division in man between his noumenal, or purely rational self, and his empirical particular self was to be overcome, namely that the worlds of nature and human history must be understood as the product of a rational purpose which achieves its goal in and through men. But this conception is for Kant only a postulate of reason.

Hegel's response to these issues is not to abandon the attempt to understand how absolute value can be realized in and through individuals, but on the contrary his aim, in common with the other German idealists, is to complete the Kantian programme by showing that the self-determination of a free rational will is actual in nature and history. The free rational will is to be understood as an infinite Spirit that realizes its absolute value in coming to see in the world of particulars a structure which is purely rational because purely the product of its drive to realize its own inherently free nature. In so knowing itself, it knows itself as the creator and sustainer of the world, as that through which all particular existence has value. But this infinite Spirit is not a pre-modern creative principle external to man. It is in the individual's fully developed self-consciousness that it achieves this self-knowledge. The individual sees himself, not as a particular product of a divine life that is not himself, but he sees his particular life as a vehicle for his own self-realization as infinite Spirit.

My aim is to express this idea of the realization of absolute value in an individual self-consciousness in ethical terms, that is in terms of the relation of the individual to the community. Hegel's ethical thought is only part of his whole philosophical system, but, since the aspirations of the whole are present in the development of its parts, it is possible to show what Hegel's ethical conception is and what I take to be unsatisfactory in it, without attempting an account of all the parts of the system.

The Philosophy of Right begins with an account of the concept of an absolutely free will considered abstractly, and then proceeds in the body of the work to the demonstration of how such a will is actual in the world. Hegel follows Kant's account of free will as the self-determination of a purely rational will, but holds that we can understand such self-determination of pure reason only insofar as we see it as realized in and through the finite, empirical wills of particular determinate beings. The free will, Hegel tells us, is the unity of two moments, the universal and the particular. The first, or universal, moment is the will understood as unlimited and infinite. If there is to be such a thing as free will, it must be unlimited by anything outside itself. It is expressed in the pure thought of oneself in abstraction from all content. It is the 'element of pure indeterminacy or that pure reflection of the ego into itself which involves the dissipation of every restriction and every content' (5).[1] The free will cannot be identified with this or that determinate content, since the very limitation to such a content denies its unrestricted nature. Yet to be real it needs to have a determinate particular content and thus the second, or particular, moment is necessary for the concept. This is the moment of finitude and limitation (6). But simply as determinate and particular, the will is limited and not free. Thus neither moment in itself is a satisfactory understanding of free will. It must be understood consequently as a unity of both moments,

---

[1] References in brackets are to paragraph numbers in the edition of the *Philosophy of Right* by T. M. Knox, Clarendon Press, 1952.

that is to say, as a will, which is inherently universal and un-limited but which realizes its nature only in and through its unity with a particular finite will. This, Hegel says, is individu-ality (7). It is the embodiment of the universal and infinite will in the particular will of a finite human being.

This appears merely to state what must be the case if the Kantian opposition between the pure rational will and the em-pirical will of individuals is to be overcome. The two must be understood as a unity. But how is this unity even conceivable? Hegel's view is that the particular finite will is itself the creation of the universal and infinite will, so that, although the particular will appears alien and opposite to the universal's true nature, the alienation and opposition is undertaken by the universal as a necessary element in its own self-realization. The universal goes out of itself in this way into the world of finitude, because what it seeks in this process is itself, the actualization of its own nature, namely freedom. This requires the activity of self-determination. Its freedom cannot be given immediately but must be achieved as a result of its own activity. The universal and free will, to be a will, must have a determinate content, but at the same time that content must be the determination of its own nature. In going out of itself into finitude as a particular will, it seeks a particular content that is adequate to its own inherent nature as universal and infinite. In the willing of such a determinate content the goal of the process of alienation will have been achieved, for the content or object of the universal will will be nothing but itself. It is thus solely self-related, and in this self-relation its inherently free nature is fully developed. It is then 'by itself without qualification, [and is] related to nothing except itself and so is released from every tie of depen-dence on anything else' (23). Freedom realized is to be under-stood as 'the free will which wills the free will' (27).

This determinate content, which is nothing but the free will's self-realized nature, is in ethical terms a system of purely rational but substantive laws and institutions. The forms of ethical life specified in the Philosophy of Right. Such a set of rational laws eluded Kant, as we have seen, for he was unable to show how such laws could be derived by pure reason. Hegel thinks he can show how this is possible. He thinks he can show that the specified ethical forms are posited or demanded by the activity of pure reason itself in its drive to realize its nature. The forms must be seen as a potential inherent in the universal and infinite will, and the drive of pure reason to realize itself is the drive to actualize this potential by giving it full expression as the forms of life of an actual world, and in so doing to know itself as an absolutely free will.

The proof of this thesis must then be a demonstration that a unique system of ethical laws can be derived by the activity of pure thought. This is to be achieved by the method of dialectic. But the dialectic is not so much the method of philosophical argument as the activity of pure reason itself in giving expression to its own nature. Dialectical thought *is* the movement of pure reason in developing the rational forms of its own being out of itself. It is the self-development of the concept, as Hegel calls it, or in ethical terms the self-determination of the will.

The movement of the dialectic is powered in the sphere of practical reason by the alienation of pure reason in a finite will and its attempt to find itself in such finitude. Thus what it seeks in such an embodiment in finitude, as we have seen, is an understanding of its existence in a particular will in which it is not limited by anything alien. The movement of thought is produced by the inadequacy of the initial conceptualizations of this unity of the universal and particular, or in other words of individuality. The initial conceptualizations fail to integrate adequately the phenomena of particularity with the universal, and so fail to overcome the universal's alienation from itself in the particular. Thought is thus driven on to develop more and more complex conceptualizations. Since each step in this development is the self-development of the concept, it constitutes a necessary form in which free will realizes itself. In itself an earlier form is an inadequate embodiment of free will, but, as a step in the universal's self-unfolding, it cannot be cancelled by the development of more adequate forms, but must be preserved as a necessary element in the complex whole. Thus the initial embodiment of free will is conceived as the will of single, independent persons, and, while this individualist conception of free will turns out to be inadequate, the freedom of independent personality, and its attendant rights, must be preserved as an element in the full attainment of freedom in a larger whole, a community. The whole, in which the free will realizes itself, is the embodied system of categories or forms of free will, which are developed by pure thought in its drive to realize itself.

In the description of the goal of free will as the discovery of a determinate content to its will, in which it finds nothing but itself, there is a certain ambiguity. The direct content, as I said, consists in the end in a structure of concepts, forms of Right or rational laws, and this appears to leave out of account a lower level of particularity that is necessary for the existence of such forms, namely the particular lives of finite men, their particular desires and wants for themselves. If the will is to overcome its necessary alienation in such finitude, particular individuality must be incorporated within the whole, which is the free will's self-realization. But this does not involve for Hegel the requirement that the particular desires of this or that man can be shown to be fully rational. At this level an ultimate arbitrariness and irrationality in finite particularity remains. Yet this whole realm of particularity is itself to be understood as the creation of pure reason, since reason's alienation in it is necessary to its own self-realization. Hence as a whole it is rationally necessary, but that this or that particular individual with this or that desire exist is an ultimately arbitrary and contingent matter.[2] What is rational is only the forms of being into which pure reason organizes finite particularity. However the otherness of this particularity is overcome for the free will, when it is willed as the necessary means through which the rational forms of freedom are actualized. Thus when finite men come to pursue their particular lives as such means to the realization of the universal in them, 'the will is then universal, because all restriction and all particular individuality has been absorbed within it' (24).

Hegel's solution to the problem of freedom, then, depends

[2] See the Preface to the *Philosophy of Right*, pp. 10–11.

on the above metaphysical interpretation of the unity of the universal and infinite will and the particular will. It involves seeing the latter as the product of the former in its drive to realize itself. This, Hegel says, is 'the innermost secret of all speculation. . . this ultimate spring of all activity, life and consciousness' (Remark to 7). This metaphysical interpretation appears to claim that what lies behind and realizes itself in the world of nature and men is a supra-human agency, an infinite spirit. But the universal will as infinite spirit is supra-human only in the sense that it transcends particular men's finitude. It is not something other than the human individual realizing the absolute value inherent in himself as a free being. To understand himself as a free individual is to understand himself as realizing a purely rational will in his particular life, and is to see his particular life as a vehicle for the realization of this higher will in him.

My claim, then, that Hegel's solution to the alienation of the particular from the universal involves an ultimate absorption and negation of particular individuality, could only be valid *as a criticism* if the above metaphysical interpretation that requires it were invalid. This I am hardly in a position to show. Within this limitation my aim will be to argue that although Hegel claims, in accordance with the principle of modernity, to have preserved the right of particular individuality to express itself fully, his account of the ultimate absorption of particular individuality within the universal negates this claim. To do this I must first give a sketch of the dialectical deduction of the forms of ethical life. For only thus can one see how the above abstractly described scheme is supposed to work, and how particular individuality is supposed to be developed in the system.

We are concerned with the attempt to find a particular existent in which an absolutely free will can realize itself fully. An existent embodying the free will is what Hegel calls Right (29). Hence the quest is for fully adequate forms of Right.

We begin with the simplest and most immediate conceptualization of right as the right of independent personality according to which the individual conceives himself as essentially and immediately free in his singular existence (35). This is the individualist's position. Such a will has in itself a purely subjective existence in relation to an external world of nature, and this subjectivity constitutes a limitation on the free will's drive to find an adequate embodiment for itself in the world. Hence the right of personality is necessarily a right to appropriate that world as its own as a means of its self-realization, i.e. a right to property (39). The right of personality, and its objectification in property and subsequently in contract, is in this way established as a necessary element in the free will's self-realization. However unsatisfactory the right of personality is as an embodiment of free will, it is still a necessary condition of free will's self-realization. The free will can be fully objectified only in and through the wills of human individuals, who recognize themselves to be, and who enjoy the rights of, persons.

These rights are inadequate embodiments of what is inherently universal essentially for the reason that the particular content of the wills of persons is not itself determined by the universal, but falls outside it. Since the self-subsistent person conceives himself to be free by the mere fact of his existence as a person, he thinks he is free whatever the particular content of his will. Hence the particular content is not itself aimed at a universal end, but at satisfying whatever the person desires. This is shown in the fact that there is no way in which a multitude of human individuals, whose particular wills are determined by their own interest, can overcome adequately their reciprocal externality. The right of contract is an attempt to do this, since in contract a common will is created between the contracting parties, and each comes to hold his property, not through a direct relation of himself to the world as in private appropriation, but through the mediation of the other's will (71). But what is expressed in this common will is not the universal itself, but only the contingent unity of particular wills in pursuit of mutual advantage (75). It is not a universal will, because a common self-consciousness is not produced through the particular determination of the contract. The purely contingent unity of particular wills in contract is revealed in the inherent possibility of a particular will finding the contract no longer advantageous to it, and hence in the breach of the contract by it, and so in wrong-doing. Wrong-doing expresses the opposition between the particular content of a free will and another particular content. This shows that the free will cannot be adequately expressed in a multitude of self-subsistent persons, since this leads to a position in which one embodiment of itself contradicts another such embodiment. It cannot see itself in both and must deny the validity of one. But it can do so only by moving on to a different and higher conception of its embodiment, namely in the moral will, in which the particular content of the will is conceived to be valid only in so far as it corresponds with the requirements of Right, or in other words with the universal itself (104).

We are still concerned with the free will's embodiment in single human wills, but the individual no longer conceives himself to be free immediately, but only in so far as he himself determines the content of his will in accordance with what is universally valid, that is to say in accordance with what is objectively good. The moral will is, thus, a self-determining will, for it involves the idea of a pure self that determines its own content (107). But the trouble with the moral will lies in the fact that the objectively good, which is the necessary aim of its particular willing, is only something demanded, an ought-to-be, and hence something distinct from the moral will itself. This results from the nature of the moral will as the will of single individuals. The good aimed at must be determined by the individual will on his own or as such. But there is no way in which this abstract conception of the good will as a pure individual will aimed at the good can yield a substantive and objective content. It is in effect the Kantian conception of the good will, the emptiness of which we have already noted (135).

In the sphere of morality we are concerned with what Hegel calls the right of the subjective will. It is the right of the individual to determine the particular content of his will himself, and to be held responsible only for what he has so determined

(107). This right has a two-fold aspect: firstly it is the right to welfare. As we are concerned with particular human subjects, whose particularity involves their own interests and welfare, the free will as embodied in the particular must involve the right of the particular individual to pursue his welfare as a necessary element in the good (121). Since this right to welfare is the right of the human subject as such, then everybody has the right, and the good that the individual must aim at is not his own welfare, but the universal welfare (125). However, welfare as an end without qualification can be incompatible with the requirements of abstract right, i.e. the right of property understood as the embodiment of self-subsistent personality, and similarly abstract right in itself is opposed to welfare. The good that we must pursue, therefore, must be a unity of right and welfare, the good of a whole which limits right and welfare in relation to each other by determining their respective claims (130).

This good is the object aimed at in the subjective will's determining on a particular content. It knows that as a free will it must determine this content itself, and thus, in the second place, the right of the subjective will is a right of conscience to be required to do only what it recognizes as the good. This is the formal right of conscience (132). It is formal only because, while true in its form, its content in the sphere of morality is not adequate to the form. It is not the single individual as such who has this right but the individual only in so far as he thinks himself as the will of an ethical community (Remark to 132).

The crucial problem still remains that the good, even though correctly conceived as a whole comprising right and welfare, is wholly indeterminate and incapable of adequate embodiment in the particular wills of *single individuals*. What we have is, on the one hand, the objective good as the object aimed at, but wholly abstract and indeterminate, and on the other hand the subjective will, which knows that it has the right to determine that content, which knows that it is free only in so far as it does determine it, but having no way of producing that content out of itself. The result is the inherent possibility of evil (139).

The subjective will in pursuing its right to determine the content of the good for itself, and having to resolve on something particular, chooses some particular that is not the good but which it sets up as such. In this case we see that a particular will, which claims to be an embodiment of the universal and is inherently the universal, contradicts the universal. And in this very awareness of contradiction we grasp that the subjective will is not something distinct from the universal which is aimed at, but is itself that universal, and hence that the objective good and the subjective will are identical. But we have already seen that the objective good is the good of a whole which delimits the respective claims of right and welfare. Since this good is now apprehended as identical with the subjective will, we see that the self realization of free will as the subjective will is identical with the realization of the good of a whole, i.e. a community of individuals. Thus the self-realization of free will is the self-realization of the will of a community in the determination of its good in an order which specifies a system of right and welfare, but only in and through the wills of its members (141).

This is Ethical life. It is the concept of freedom actualized. The free will is to be understood as the mind of a community, which gives itself actuality in a particular content in which it recognizes itself as free and unrestricted because the content is nothing but the specific determinations of itself in purely rational laws and institutions. Thus 'the ethical order has been represented by mankind as eternal justice, as gods absolutely existent, in contrast with which the empty business of individuals is only a game of see-saw' (Addition to 145). It is only in so far as the individual is the vehicle of this order's existence that he has significance and attains his freedom. In conforming his will to the ethical order 'he recognizes as the end which moves him to act the universal which is itself unmoved but is disclosed in its specific determinations as rationality actualized. He knows that his own dignity and the whole stability of his particular ends are grounded in this same universal, and it is therein that he actually attains these' (152).

But this self-actualization is possible only in and through the wills of its members, in so far as they recognize in their willing the will of the community realizing itself. At the same time the self-realization of the concept of free will as the will of a community is not supposed to be the denial of the individuality of the community's members. It is not supposed to reduce them simply to a means by which this supra-individual will realizes itself, as though they were nothing but parts of a larger whole. For the whole only constitutes itself in their consciousness, and is identical with the individual's will. The individual member when willing his *particular life* as the means to the self-realization of the whole, nevertheless identifies himself in that act as the whole. His freedom and individuality consists in his grasping in his person a unity of absolute value with particular life. This is satisfied in so far as in his particular life as a member of the community fulfilling a particular function within it, that which has absolute value, namely an absolutely free will, is identical with, and has actuality as, his will.

As a *particular finite being*, the individual is related to the ethical order as accident to substance (145). 'Whether the individual exists or not is all one to the objective ethical order. It alone is permanent and is the power regulating the life of individuals' (Addition to 145).

The concept of freedom develops itself as ethical life in an order of institutions which constitute the purely rational substantive forms of the concept's existence. These forms are the family, civil society, and state. To complete the self-development of the concept, then, we need to demonstrate the rationality of these institutions. The concept has developed itself as a unity of the objective order of a community with a subjective will, namely as the order of a community which exists as identical with the wills of its members. We are now looking for an adequate embodiment of this concept, and the simplest and most immediate conceptualization of this unity is that of a family. The unity of a family is immediately realized in the particular wills of its members, in the sense that the member of the family, in his family activities, acts directly as a family member and for the family's good, which he sees as identical with his own good. He does not distinguish his own particular aims from the good of the whole and seek to realize them (158).

This is an unsatisfactory embodiment of the ethical idea since the individual is in the family as a pure member and cannot develop his particular individuality through it. He needs to pursue the development of his personality as an independent entity and for this he must throw off the shackles of the family, and affirm his freedom as a self-subsistent personality, by which he makes himself his own end. The particular family is thus destroyed by the departure of the children in search of their self-development as free individuals. For this the institutions of civil society are necessary.

At this point we return to the rights of personality, private property and contract, only now no longer conceived abstractly, but as an order in which the mind of a community is realizing itself. Civil society is an ethical whole, but in it the right of the particular has its full development. Hence while it is in fact the mind of the whole that is being realized through the full development of particular personality, the whole is not present to the consciousness of its members (181). Civil society thus involves the right of the particular individual to pursue his own private interest and needs in the course of the development and satisfaction of his personality. In appearance civil society is, in the first place, a sphere in which only private ends are pursued. But in the pursuit of his interest the individual has to enter into exchange relations with others, and so can only attain his ends through a scheme of cooperation which makes him dependent on others. He is dependent on a whole economic and legal system which provides him with opportunities and protects his rights. At the same time this whole is itself determined through individuals' pursuit of private interest (182–7).

Civil society is in the first instance a world in which private ends alone are pursued, and individuals see their relation to others and to the whole as the means by which their private ends can be attained, yet the underlying reality is the reverse of this, and the truth is that the pursuit of private ends is the means by which the whole is developed. In civil society the truth of the particular individual's functions in the whole cannot be completely comprehended, nevertheless he is partially educated to a grasp of this truth through his membership of the ethical forms that are produced in civil society, primarily classes and corporations. In the course of individuals' pursuit of private interest and the consequent interrelation of activities, an 'entire complex is built up into particular systems of needs, means and types of work relative to these needs, modes of satisfaction and of theoretical and practical education, i.e. into systems, to one or other of which individuals are assigned – in other words into class-divisions' (201). By coming to see himself as a member of a class (to which, in fact, despite the above quotation, Hegel requires that the individual assign himself, not be assigned, see 206) the individual now comes to have as his end, through his private activity, the maintenance of himself as a member (207). Furthermore, as a member of the business class (the others being the agricultural class and the universal class of civil servants), the individual will be a member of a corporation. Corporations are organizations of the common interests of particular branches of business activity (251), and by becoming a member of one the individual 'belongs to a whole which is itself an organ of the entire society, and . . . is actively concerned in promoting the comparatively disinterested end of this whole' (253). It is not that the individual as member ceases to pursue what he identified before as his private interest, but that he now sees that interest as not something private to him, but as a means by which this higher end is established and realized.

Yet corporations and the other ethical elements in civil society are not adequate conceptualizations of the relation of particular individuality to the whole. For this the conceptualization of ethical life as the state is necessary. The state is the whole community, comprehending family and civil society, come to consciousness of itself in the wills of its members in and through political institutions.

The state is the actuality of concrete freedom. But concrete freedom consists in this, that personal individuality and its particular interests not only achieve their complete development and gain explicit recognition for their right (as they do in the sphere of the family and civil society) but, for one thing, they also pass over of their own accord into the interest of the universal, and for another thing, they know and will the universal; they even recognize it as their own substantive mind; they take it as their end and aim and are active in its pursuit. The result is that the universal does not prevail or achieve completion except along with particular interests and through the cooperation of particular knowing and willing; and individuals likewise do not live as private persons for their own ends alone, but in the very act of willing these they will the universal in the light of the universal, and their activity is consciously aimed at none but the universal end. The principle of modern states has prodigious strength and depth because it allows the principle of subjectivity to progress to its culmination in the extreme of self-subsistent personal particularity, and yet at the same time brings it back to the substantive unity and so maintains this unity in the principle of subjectivity itself (260).

The essential function of the pursuit of private interest in civil society is that it is only through the individual's attempt to realize a conception of himself as free as a self-subsistent particular person that he can come to understand his dependence on the whole, and thus that he is not adequately free as a private person, but only as a bearer of the life of the whole. Men can only grasp the true conditions of their freedom by first developing private aims in themselves, and subsequently being brought back to the universal through the ethical elements in civil society and state. And, as has already been emphasized, this return to the universal does not cancel private interest, but changes it into a particular function of the life of a larger self-determining will. In the state the concept of free will is actualized because the unity of the universal with the particular is achieved in so far as the individual sees the realization of his particular ends as identical with the realization of universal ends, since the former are the means by which the latter are established.

Yet however much Hegel proclaims the necessity for the full development of particular individuality as the means to the self-realization of an absolutely free will, individuality, understood as the value residing in specific persons, is destroyed in his system. By individuality Hegel means the unity of a particular empirical will with a universal will. The universal will in ethical life is the will of the community, so that when the human individual says 'I' with full ethical self-consciousness, he means that an impersonal, communal self is speaking in and through his empirical particular nature. As a particular being, the human individual develops his particular life in the pursuit of his interests, as these are determined and modified by his existence in, and education by, civil society. But the value of this particular life lies in its existence as the necessary means to the realization of the absolute value that resides in the universal. Thus as a particular the individual has value only as a means to something else. This something else is the universal realizing itself in him. But in this respect the individual is not this specific person, but an impersonal self, the community speaking in him. Thus the individual, as this person, has no value as an end in Hegel's thought. As this person, the individual is merely a means.

This devaluation of the particular is evident in many places; for example, in the remark on sexual love in relation to marriage: 'those works of modern art, dramatic and other, in which the love between the sexes is the main interest, are pervaded by a chill despite the heat of passion they portray, for they associate passion with accident throughout and represent the entire dramatic interest as if it rested solely on the characters as *these individuals* (i.e. particular individuals); what rests on them may indeed be of infinite importance to *them*, but is of none whatever in itself' (Remark to 162). What is of importance is that in their particular lives the rational form of the family be given existence.

The attack on the particular is clearest in Hegel's rational deduction of war as a necessary element in the realization of absolute value.

The state is a particular individual among others, and as such it contains an alien element of contingency and arbitrariness which ensures its finitude and death. This 'engagement with chance events coming from without', through which the existence of the state is put at risk, however, expresses the state's actual infinity, that is to say 'its absolute power against everything individual and particular (within itself) against life, property and their rights, even against societies and associations'. In other words it is in conflict with other states, and hence in war and in the sacrifice war requires, that the ultimate unimportance of the particular individual is given full expression. 'War is the state of affairs which deals in earnest with the vanity of temporal goods and concerns. . .this is what makes it the moment in which the ideality of the particular attains its right and is actualized' (Remark to 324). The ideality of the particular here means the existence of the particular not for itself, but only as a moment in the life of the infinite. The right of the particular, which is actualized in war, is its right to serve, through self-sacrifice, as the means by which the ethical substance of the state is preserved.

Hegel says in a passage from which I have already quoted that 'whether the individual exists or not is all one to the objective ethical order' (addition to 145). But this does not mean that it is unimportant to the ethical order whether individuals satisfy their particular interests or not. The ethical standpoint can be educated to self-consciousness in individuals only through their coming to see how their particular interests are satisfied in and through the whole. This must continue to be the case if the unity of the universal and particular is to be maintained. Yet all that is necessary is that those particulars who exist find their satisfaction in the whole. It is of no importance to the whole who these particulars are, or what the details of their particular lives may be. They exist purely in order that, through the pursuit of their particular interests, rational forms of social life may be developed, in the willing of which by individuals the communal self realizes itself.

Given that the members of the community must find their particular satisfaction in serving the whole, there must be a perfect harmony of particular interests with each other in the whole for this condition to be satisfied. This is, indeed, the inherent aspiration of the free will in its attempt to find an adequate embodiment of itself in social and political life. But Hegel is not so naive as to suppose that the modern state, whose institutions he describes, constitutes such a perfect embodiment. In the first place the insufficiency of the state is manifest in the failure of civil society to produce the desired harmony of interests. It creates within itself extremes of wealth and poverty, and is unable, despite its great resources, to secure to all the means for the development of their particular individuality.

In the second place, the state is one particular individual among others, and is as such limited by them (322). The universal and absolutely free will cannot be realized in any one state, but only in the dialectical succession of states as a world-mind that manifests itself in such a history (340). Yet it is not even in world-history that freedom is finally actual. We have to leave the realm of objective spirit altogether, that is to say, the practical world of societies and states, and grasp freedom in the theoretical realm which reaches its culmination in the pure self-activity of philosophy or dialectical thought, in which the object of thought is through and through nothing but the subject determining itself.

It is in the subordination of the practical realm of ethical life to the theoretical realm of art, religion and philosophy that the ultimate triviality of the particular's concerns is finally driven home. For, although the self-realization of spirit in self-thinking thought requires the whole preceding development of particular life, together with the ethical substance, as necessary elements of its own advance to absolute self-knowledge and self-determination, it is self-evidently not the particularity of this or that individual man or individual state that is preserved in this self-contemplation of spirit, which is the meaning and end of the world.[3]

The devaluation of the particular individual is thus a central requirement of Hegel's philosophical scheme. The individual,

[3] My implicit criticism here is not that philosophy ought to include the particularity of specific individuals, an evident absurdity, but that philosophy is not the meaning and end of the world, and hence that the value of particular individuals should not be seen as the means whereby self-thinking thought is actual.

as this person, has no value as an end, but only as a means. In this sense individuality is absorbed into and destroyed by the life of the universal. This result stems from the attempt to conceptualize the actuality of absolute freedom, together with the recognition that absolute freedom cannot exist in individuals considered in themselves, but only as their will is that of an ethical community. Hence the value of their specific lives is purely as means for this other will to exist. This conception of the value of the particular in relation to the whole is grounded in fundamentally the same idea of freedom that is present in the individualist notion. It is the idea of a self-determining will that as such is completely unrestricted by anything outside itself. It is precisely this idea that should be rejected.

MARX

In Marx's early writings one finds a criticism of individualist conceptions of the relation of the individual to society, which in some ways runs parallel to my own arguments in Part 1 of this work. Marx perceives in these conceptions a radically unsatisfactory separation and opposition between the individual as a particular directed towards his private activity and the individual as citizen concerned with the general. Consider in the first place what he says on this in his Critique of Hegel's *Philosophy of Right*.[4]

Marx claims here that Hegel's idea of the state not only involves the separation of civil society and state, but thereby divides man's existence into that of citizen on the one hand and unpolitical private man on the other. Man's particular existence in civil society appears as a content to which the political state is organizing form. But in fact the political state is only an abstract and empty idea of man's life as citizen. It has no content itself, and what content it has comes from the particular interests of civil society. Thus it claims to be the universal life and interest of man, while in fact being determined by particular interest. Against the Hegelian

[4] D. McLellan (ed.), *Karl Marx: Early Texts*, Basil Blackwell, 1971, p. 61 f.

conception, Marx puts forward the idea of democracy, which, he claims, is a real and not a formal universal. It is not a particular feature separate from its content. It is itself the whole. Hence in true democracy the state may be said to disappear, for it disappears as a separate entity. The state and law in a democracy are self-determinations of the people, a particular content of the common life.

The point hardly does justice to Hegel, since in the state, understood as the whole community (including family and civil society) determining itself through political forms, the individual is no longer, even in respect of his particular interests in civil society, an unpolitical private man, for he pursues his interests as a duty to the whole. Nevertheless, even if the criticism does not apply to Hegel, I am hardly the person to argue it applies to no one.

The main point is given more developed treatment in the later essay, *On the Jewish Question.*[5] In this essay Marx is replying to an article by Bruno Bauer who claimed that there were no grounds for the *political* emancipation of the Jews, because the emancipation of the Jews was a *religious* problem. Bauer had argued that the Jewish problem could be solved only by a religious emancipation of society, by which he meant that Jews should cease to be Jews and Christians cease to be Christians, and all should become unqualified and undifferentiated men. Jews have a claim to emancipation only as men, and this involves an abolition of their Jewishness. Marx argues, in reply, that Bauer confuses political rights with the recognition of religious groups. It is the peculiarity of the modern state that it can emancipate men politically, by recognizing them on the political level as undifferentiated and equal men, and yet leave their real identity as members of particular groups or classes unchanged. Thus man can be politically liberated and yet not be a free man.

In the rest of the essay Marx examines how this is possible. Political emancipation is an illusory promise of human freedom because it annuls private property politically, but not really in

[5] McLellan, op. cit., p. 85.

fact. It abolishes private property as a qualification for citizenship, and so for participation in the apparent common life of the people. It proclaims the political equality of man. But it leaves material life in civil society unchanged. The perfected separate political state is by its nature the communal life of man abstracted from and opposed to his material life. Man, Marx says,

> now leads a double life, a heavenly one and an earthly one, not only in thought and consciousness, but in reality, in life. He has a life both in the political community, where he is valued as a communal being, and in civil society where he is active as a private individual, treats other men as means, degrades himself to a means, and becomes the plaything of alien powers.[6]

In the modern state, as for example its main lines are delineated in the work of the French Revolution, the rights of man are distinguished from the rights of the citizen. The rights of man are his rights as a member of civil society, that is to say as egoistic private man, separated from other men and community. The freedom of man here is the right to do what one likes within limits set by the equal rights of others. The practical application of this right is private property, which is a right of selfishness. The doctrine of the rights of man does not conceive man as a communal being, but presents communal life as a framework external to private individuals, who are held together not by their common essence, but by their private need to use each other for their own ends. In Marx's view it is not political man who is real in this arrangement. He is an abstract fictional or allegorical person; it is man as member of civil society, egoistic man, who as materially real will dominate in such a society.

Marx concludes the essay with a brief statement of the requirements of emancipation. This must involve a reintegration of the abstract citizen with individual material life, in order to produce an undivided entity which is both civil society and state: Man 'as an individual man in his empirical life, in his individual work and relationships [must] become a species-

[6] McClellan, op. cit., pp. 93–4.

being: man must recognize his own forces as social forces, organize them and thus no longer separate social forces from himself in the form of political forces. Only when this has been achieved will human emancipation be completed.'[7]

We have here already a conception of the relation between the particular and general life of man which dominates all Marx's early ethical writing, and which contains the essential ethical idea of communist society, which also underlies, but is not developed, in his later work. Marx's ethical inspiration at this point comes from Feuerbach, and it will be useful to outline the latter's conception of man as species-being, which Marx largely takes over.

Feuerbach has the idea that Hegel's system contains the truth, but in a mystified form. This is true of the Christian religion also, between which and Feuerbach's materialist humanism Hegel is seen as a half-way stage. So Feuerbach offers a demystification of these systems of thought, which is to be achieved through an inversion of the fundamental subject and predicate in them.[8] Thus in respect of Hegel's system we see that the supreme creative principle or subject, that which has absolute value and is an end in itself, is pure reason, and roughly speaking that on which reason acts is man as the vehicle of reason's self-realization. However, the true subject of infinite value is man, and what he worships in God or Pure Reason is nothing other than his species' own essential powers.[9]

The affirmation of man, the species, as in effect the divine on earth is specifically intended as the affirmation of a materialist and not an idealist principle. Thus by man Feuerbach does not intend to mean a non-materialistic entity that only exists in man, for example pure reason. It is true that man is said to have certain essential powers, through which he achieves perfection and is of infinite value, and that these powers are reason, will and love. He also holds that these powers are not simply em-

[7] McLellan, op. cit., p. 108.

[8] L. Feuerbach, *The Essence of Christianity*, trans. M. Evans. J. Chapman, 1854, p. 59.

[9] ibid., p. 12.

pirical capacities of individuals. The individual is said to be nothing without them, and consequently that they govern him, rather than that he dominates them.[10] Through these powers it is the species that creates the individual. Yet none of this is supposed to be incompatible with materialism. This is because, although he uses the language of idealism, e.g. the species is the infinite, the unlimited, the perfect, that which exists for its own sake and so on, it turns out that it is the species, understood as completed in all men in past, present and future taken together, which is accorded these attributes. The history of mankind consists of a continuous and progressive conquest of limits, which indefinitely extended into the future means apparently that the species is unlimited. The perfection of the species is realized only in all men taken together. Taken as a whole they present the perfect man.[11]

Feuerbach describes man not just as a species, but as a species-being. By this he means that man and only man is conscious of his species. The animal apparently is conscious of himself as an individual, but not as a member of a species. Consequently man has a form of life, which consists in his relation to his species, that is not available to animals. This species-life or general life is man's essential nature.[12]

In order to understand what this doctrine amounts to as an ethical theory, and what its implications are in Marx's thought, we need to concentrate on the conception of individuality and on the relation of the particular individual to the whole in it. How does the individual relate to the species? Feuerbach has a general doctrine about the relations of a subject to an object, which bears on this issue. This is the claim that an object, to which a subject essentially and necessarily relates, is nothing else than the subject's own but objective nature. He gives as an example the relation of the earth to the sun: the peculiar nature of the earth is defined in terms of its relation to the sun. Thus the sun is the earth's other self, and in being related to the sun it is self-related.[13] This point is to be brought to bear on the

---

[10] ibid., p. 3. [11] ibid., pp. 154–8. [12] ibid., pp. 1–2.
[13] ibid., pp. 4–5. This seems senseless, since the earth is not a subject.

individual's relation to his species: when men use their essential powers in relation to the external, they become acquainted with their own nature as species-being. The power of the object over the individual is the power of his own nature. Whatever kind of object we are at any time conscious of, we are always at the same time conscious of our nature. It should be in this way, then, that the individual's self-consciousness as member of the species develops. But man can only arrive at this truth by first alienating himself from himself in attributing his essential nature and its creative powers to an alien being, God, and worshipping them there. The Feuerbachian unravelling of this mystification, however, allows the truth to become clear to man.

The truth is, then, that in the external, in nature and in other men, the individual apprehends his species-nature, and hence sees that both himself and the other are modes in which the species relates to itself. In the face of the other the individual recognizes his limitation and finitude, but at the same time, by seeing himself as the species in the other, becomes aware that through their combination they are the infinite. The individual must not identify himself directly with the species, but must see himself as a part of mankind and contemplate mankind as a whole. In the relation between me and the other, the other is the representative of the species for me, and has a universal significance as a deputy of mankind. Through this relation to the other I realize the community that constitutes humanity, a differentiated community by which we all complete each other.[14] In living in the consciousness of the species as a reality, the individual regards his existence for others as that existence which is one with his essence, and thus an immortal existence. He lives wholly for humanity; so how, Feuerbach asks, can he hold in reserve a special existence for himself, how can he separate himself from mankind?[15]

The trouble with this account is that at no point does it become clear in what the individual's self-consciousness as individual consists, and hence how this individuality relates to his consciousness of the whole. Indeed Feuerbach's ethical view

[14] ibid., pp. 156–7.   [15] ibid., p. 170.

wholly depends on ignoring this issue, and *assuming*, but not arguing for, the view that individual self-consciousness is unproblematic. This is shown in Feuerbach's bland attribution of *individual* self-consciousness to animals as well as men. Men are not defined by their individuality, but by their species-consciousness. Furthermore, Feuerbach specifically criticizes the Christian religion for the conception of the individual which is contained in it. In the person of Christ there is represented an immediate identity of species and individual, by which he means that the essence of humanity, its infinite value, is immediately incarnate in Christ. This is unsatisfactory because it oversteps the limits of nature and reason, and the unsatisfactoriness is manifest in the necessity of declaring this individual to be a transcendent being. The defect in Christianity lies in the absence in it of the sense that men taken together are required to constitute humanity, and not individuals as such.[16]

It becomes clear here, I think, that Feuerbach has in fact little grasp of individuality. The Christian conception of the unity of the infinite and finite in the person of Christ, is the basis of the modern individualist doctrines of Part 1 (and Hegel's transformation of them). The individualist of Part 1 holds that the individual as such is of objective value, and this involves an immediate unity of the absolute value that is present in man as such with the particular individual. The value that resides in the individual is identical with the value of the species. Hence individuality understood as the particular being's consciousness of himself as containing such value is identical with his consciousness of himself as a member of humanity. It is this idea that Feuerbach, without being at all clear what he is doing, is rejecting. Let us suppose with Feuerbach that absolute value resides in humanity. How is consciousness of this absolute value constituted? The particular individual becomes conscious that he has value only as part of the species which has absolute value. Since he can only see himself as a part *he* cannot constitute in his consciousness the value of the whole. For were he to do so,

[16] ibid., p. 153.

141

he would not simply be a part of the whole, but at the same time the whole would lie immediately in him. There would be an immediate identity of the whole and the individual, mediated by the part in the whole which he occupies. The individual must have a two-fold dimension to his value.

Let us now return to Marx. In the two works we have already considered we have the idea of an essential human nature which is social, from which man alienates himself by separating this essence off from his particular activity, so that he fails to identify this activity as the activity of his essential nature, but on the contrary identifies it as his purely private activity. In the *Economic and Philosophical Manuscripts* Marx gives us an account of what the essential human powers are, how they become alienated, and what the overcoming of this alienation will involve. The essential human power is labour, labour as a productive and creative activity. This power is manifest in a relation to nature. By labouring on the external, nature, the individual develops his essential human power and is related to nature as to his own essence. Thus man realizes himself through the production of objects from nature in which he can see his human essence objectified. Alienation is the inability to relate to the object of labour in this way. The root of alienated labour lies in the alienation of the worker in the act of production through the sale of his labour to another (or of course through his enslavement). The object of the worker's labour is thus appropriated by another, and the worker is left not with a relation to this object, but a relation to what he gets through the sale of his labour, subsistence wages. His object in his work becomes self-interest, the purely private.

In alienated labour the individual is alienated from his productive activity as expressive of his essential power, from his product as objectification of this power, from nature as the embodiment of his human essence, from his species and from other men. Man, for Marx, is a species being in that 'he makes both his own and other species into his objects, but also, and this is only another way of putting the same thing, he relates to himself as to the present, living species in that he relates to himself as to a universal and free being'.[17] By this he means that the individual sees in his activity the activity of the species, and in pursuing his own ends is thereby pursuing the ends of the species. The whole character of a species is given by its manner of productive life or vital activity. The species-characteristic of man is free conscious productive activity. That is to say, 'man makes his vital activity itself into an object of his will and consciousness'.[18] But he is only a free conscious being, and his own life is only an object to him, because he is a species-being and hence sees in the objects of his individual activity a universal end. However, in ceasing to have as his end in his productive activity the realization of the species life, he is alienated from it. He is at the same time alienated from other men as particular beings, since he relates to them as to means to his selfish ends and not as to manifestations of species-life.

In Feuerbach's ethical thought the individual recognizes the species to be active in and through his particular life and that of others. The universality and freedom of the species lies in the combination of the parts to complete the whole. In Marx this idea is expressed through the running together of the idea of the essentially social nature of the individual's productive activity, the fact that it is the conscious realization of species-powers, with that of the cooperative character of production. Thus the individual realizes the species only in part, and the realization of the whole requires the combination of these parts. This idea is most fully expressed in manuscript notes on James Mill's thought written in the same year as the *Economic and Philosophical Manuscripts*.

Exchange, both of human activity within production itself and also of human products with each other, *is equivalent to* species-activity and species enjoyment whose real, conscious and true being is *social* activity and *social* enjoyment. Since human nature is the true communal nature of man, men create and produce their communal nature by their natural action, they produce their *social* being which is no abstract, universal power over against single individuals, but the nature of each individual, his own activity, his own life, his own enjoyment, his own wealth. Therefore this true communal nature does not originate in reflection, it

[17] D. McLellan, op. cit., p. 138.   [18] ibid., p. 139.

takes shape through the need and egoism of individuals, i.e. it is produced directly by the effect of their being. It is not dependent on man whether this communal being exists or not; but so long as man has not recognized himself as man and has not organized the world in a human way, this communal nature appears in the form of alienation, because its subject, man, is a self-alienated being. Men, not in the abstract, but as real, living, particular individuals are this nature...Therefore to say that man alienates himself is the same as to say that the society of this alienated man is a caricature of his real communal nature, his true species life, that therefore his activity appears as a suffering, his own creation appears as an alien power[19] [my emphasis].

This passage clearly recognizes that cooperation between men in production, or, as he says, the exchange of human activity in production, or of the products of such activity, is the activity of the species, which is at the same time the essentially social or communal nature of man. This communal nature, or social being, is produced naturally by men in the course of their individual productive activity, in their drive to satisfy their needs. It will nevertheless be concealed from the individual, and take on an alienated form, unless he recognizes himself as man, i.e. his true species nature, and organizes production in a human way.

In alienated production, Marx says, in the same manuscript:

I have produced for myself and not for you, as you have produced for yourself and not for me. You are as little concerned by the result of my production in itself as I am directly concerned by the result of your production. That is, our production is not a production of men for men as such, that is, social production. Thus, as a man none of us is in a position to be able to enjoy the product of another. We are not present to our mutual products as men. Thus, neither can our exchange be the mediating movement which confirms that my product is for you, because it is an objectification of your own essence, your need. For what links our productions together is not the human essence.[20]

Just as for Feuerbach the essential powers of man, which constitute the unity of men, in so far as together they form the complete expression of the species, are alienated from man in his attribution of them to an alien God to whom he enslaves

[19] ibid., pp. 193-4.   [20] ibid., p. 199.

himself, so for Marx the social essence of man is in alienated production attributed to an alien thing, money.

The essence of money is not, to begin with that it constitutes the external-ization of property, but that the mediating activity or movement, the human social act whereby man's products complete each other, is alienated, and becomes the property of a material being outside man, money. By externalizing this mediating activity itself, man has now lost himself and becomes sub-human, man's relationship to things and his activity with them becomes the activity of a being outside and above man...His slavery thus arrives at its culmination. It is clear that this mediator has now become a real god.[21]

To produce in a fully human manner, Marx says, involves the following double affirmation of oneself and one's fellow-men:

I would have (1) objectified in my production my individuality and its peculiarity and thus both in my activity enjoyed an individual expression of my life and also in looking at the object have had the individual pleasure of realizing that my personality was objective, visible to the senses and thus a power raised beyond all doubt. (2) In your enjoyment or use of my product I would have had the direct enjoyment of realizing that I had both satisfied a human need by my work and also objectified the human essence and therefore fashioned for another human being the object that met his need. (3) I would have been for you the mediator between you and the species and thus been acknowledged and felt by you as a completion of your own essence and a necessary part of yourself and have thus realized that I am confirmed both in your thought and in your love. (4) In my expression of your life, and thus in my own activity have realized my own essence, my human, my communal essence.[22]

In this passage we have a much clearer account of what human productive activity consists in after the overcoming of alienation and the abolition of private property than in those passages of the *Economic and Philosophical Manuscripts* which directly describe this. Nevertheless, some attention must be paid to the latter. Firstly, it is the positive abolition of private property that is the central requirement in the overcoming of alienation. It is this which allows for the re-appropriation of the human social essence by man, and 'the return of man out of religion, family, state, etc. into his human, i.e. social being'.[23]

[21] ibid., p. 189.   [22] ibid., p. 202.   [23] ibid., p. 149.

Secondly, the individual productive activity whose social essence is to be recovered under communism is not necessarily immediately cooperative in the sense in which two men cutting down a tree together are engaged in cooperative effort. 'Even if my activity is a scientific one etc. an activity that I can seldom perform directly in company with other men, I am still acting socially since I am acting as a man.'[24] The material of the scientist's activity is a social product, as indeed is language for the thinker. But also the individual's 'own existence is social activity; therefore what I individually produce, I produce individually for society, conscious of myself as a social being'.[25]

As we have seen, Feuerbach's conception of the individual as species-being involves no adequate grasp of the nature of individuality, treating individual self-consciousness as an unproblematic consequence of his particular existence. If Marx's inspiration in these early humanist writings is essentially Feuerbachian, we should find that Marx has no better grasp of individuality. This is so. Consider the following passages on individuality.

It is above all necessary to avoid restoring society as a fixed abstraction opposed to the individual. The individual is the social being...the individual and the species-life of man are not different, although, necessarily the mode of existence of individual life is a more particular or a more general mode of species-life or the species-life is a more particular or more general individual life...

However much he is a particular individual (and it is precisely his particularity that makes him an individual and a truly individual communal being) man is just as much the totality, the ideal totality, the subjective existence of society as something thought and felt...

Death appears as the harsh victory of the species over the particular individual and seems to contradict their unity; but the particular individual is only a determinate species-being and thus mortal.[26]

The recurrent claim is that the individual is the social being, that there cannot be any separation between them, and that the individual's particularity consists in his being a particular mode of existence of the species or general or social life. It follows that for Marx individual self-consciousness is unproblematic.

[24] ibid., p. 150.   [25] ibid., p. 150.   [26] ibid., pp. 150–1.

The problematic nature of individuality consists in this, that to possess individuality is to become conscious of one's single existence as a self-constituted whole, and as an end to be valued by the self (in or for itself). To achieve this self-consciousness, it is necessary to separate oneself off from others and establish oneself as an independent whole. In the process one has alienated oneself from the larger social whole, and created the problem of the nature of one's relations to it. The unproblematic nature of individuality for Feuerbach and Marx means that for them the individual to be conscious of his single existence in the world does not have to constitute himself as an end in the first place apart from others. His individual self-consciousness arises quite unproblematically, and in an unalienated state of the world will naturally express itself as a consciousness that his individual ends are at the same time and ipso facto social ends, and that there cannot be any division or conflict between them. To conceive oneself as an individual in the world is to distinguish oneself from others, but at the same time to see that self and others are both modes of social activity and thus that each complements the other as part of the whole.

But what is the self that conceives itself as an individual and as social activity? It is that which constitutes the individual as a whole in himself, and in conceiving itself also as a species-being must constitute in its individual consciousness the unity of that larger whole.

It is, of course, true that for both Feuerbach and Marx this immediate unity of individual and social consciousness is arrived at only through the alienation of the human essence in religion or in private production and exchange. But the alienation is not an experience that each individual in every generation must undergo to create his individuality and continuously reconstitute the social whole. It is experienced only historically and overcome once and for all with the establishment of humanist or socialist society.

The Feuerbachian–Marxist assumption that individuality and sociality are, in an unalienated state of the world, immediately one, must be said in the end to be an incredible facile, not to say juvenile, conception. It fails to grasp the most obvious nature and conditions of existence of individuality, and any attempt to realize it in the world through coercive power will be destructive only of the moral value that it purports to be realizing.

The failure to allow for individuality is manifest in Marx's espousal of communism. Communism is not a clearly defined mode of social organization. It is the purely negative abolition of private forms of social life and their consequences, the family, private property and the separate organization of the state. Marx cannot say what is to be put in their place other than in the first instance crude forms of collective life, the communal ownership of women and property. This is to be superseded by the full realization of man's social being, but what this involves is described only in general terms of what it is to produce in a human manner, which I have quoted above. It describes no specific form of life. This is not surprising, because the idea that underlies communism, man's communal essence, is nothing other than the denial that the recognition of the *claims* of individuals for their own particular lives is a necessary element in social life. But since social life and its forms are inherently grounded in the drive of particular individuals to satisfy themselves, the denial of individuals' claims involves the denial that any forms are necessary. As we have seen above, Marx accepts that social life springs from the drives of particular individuals, but, because of his denial of the claims of individuality, he commits himself, whether he knows it fully or not, to an utterly formless social life.

The relation of the early Marx to Feuerbach is clear enough, and is expressed by him in a letter to the latter in which he says that Feuerbach has provided the philosophic basis for socialism and communism. 'The unity of man with man based on the real differences between men, the concept of human species transferred from the heaven of abstraction to the real earth, what is this other than the concept of society!'[27] Yet Marx subsequently criticized Feuerbach, and, it is often claimed, abandoned his early ethical humanism for a solidly based scientific

[27] ibid., p. 184.

socialism developed in his historical and economic analyses. It is undoubtedly true that his mature work is devoted to historical and economic analysis in which we find expressed very little of the earlier ideas on alienation and on the social essence of individual activity. Nevertheless, there are famous passages in *Capital* vol. i in which these earlier ideas re-appear as clear as could be, and they frequently recur in the unpublished manuscript of his mature period known as the *Grundrisse*.[28] Furthermore, there is no incompatibility between the earlier conceptions of the social nature of man and the later historical materialism. Since, throughout his mature work, he conceives revolutionary socialism to involve a liberation of humanity, and fails to provide any new philosophical and ethical account of what this is, it is reasonable to assume that his earlier account of the social essence of man is to be transferred into his later theory.

Consider first what his criticism of Feuerbach is. In the theses on Feuerbach, as in the opening section of *The German Ideology*, Marx criticizes Feuerbach, and the left Hegelians generally, for grounding their supposedly materialist humanism ultimately in a theoretical view of the world. To change the world by overcoming alienation, for the left Hegelians, it was necessary only to arrive at the correct conception theoretically, i.e. to reinterpret the world, and everything would fall into place. As an alternative Marx offers the idea of revolutionary practice. But in this conception it should be noted that he does not seriously criticize the theoretical content of the idea of man's essence. The *6th thesis* appears to contradict this claim, for it consists in a criticism of Feuerbach's conception of the individual and of the human essence. It goes thus:

Feuerbach resolves the religious essence into the *human* essence. But the human essence is no abstraction inherent in each single individual. In its reality it is the ensemble of the social relations.

Feuerbach, who does not enter upon a criticism of this real essence, is consequently compelled:

---

[28] See D. McLellan (ed.), *Marx's Grundrisse*, Macmillan, 1971. The passages in *Capital* I discuss below, pp. 151–3.

1. To abstract from the historical process and to fix the religious sentiment as something by itself, and to presuppose an abstract – *isolated* – human individual.

2. The human essence, therefore, can with him be comprehended only as genus, as an internal, dumb generality which merely *naturally* unites the many individuals.[29]

This looks as though it is a criticism of Feuerbach for holding that the human essence is an abstraction inherent in each individual, and thus his individual is the abstract, isolated man who contains the human essence in himself; whereas the truth is, as Marx affirms, that the human essence is the ensemble of social relations. But if this is Marx's criticism here, it is evidently a travesty of Feuerbach's ethical thought. For it is precisely Feuerbach who rejected the abstract conception of the individual as a being containing the human essence in his single or isolated existence. The point of the doctrine that man is a species-being is to affirm that the individual's humanity is realized only in his relations to others. Feuerbach could assert as validly as Marx that the human essence is the ensemble of men's relations. Thus Marx's point here, appearances to the contrary notwithstanding, does not involve a rejection of the ethical doctrine of his early period, which he had correctly attributed to Feuerbach.[30]

The *6th thesis* culminates in the criticism that for Feuerbach the human essence only *naturally* unites the many individuals. What Marx opposes to this natural unity is, of course, unification through revolutionary practice. It is certainly true of Feuerbach that human unity is inherent in the nature of human consciousness and its powers, so that man has only to understand himself and his species-powers correctly for this unity to be achieved. Thus there is no revolutionary-practical criticism of the real essence of man. This is Marx's major point in the

[29] L. S. Feuer (ed.), *Marx and Engels: Basic Writings*, Fontana Library, 1969, p. 285.

[30] Of course, it is possible that Marx mistakenly believed that he had rejected his early ethical position in criticizing Feuerbach. His confusion on this point would perhaps explain his reluctance to engage in ethical theorizing in his later work.

theses as a whole, and if it is the main point in the *6th thesis* as well, then once again it does not involve a criticism of the early ethical conception of man's social essence.

The real issue between them would, then, be as to how this conception is produced in man's consciousness. Marx claims that for Feuerbach it is produced by pure thought, a claim which destroys Feuerbach's pretensions to a materialist theory. For Marx the conception is produced in the course of man's changing the world, and must be being produced in reality before it can be apprehended in thought, or rather is apprehended in thought in the course of its production in reality. Thus any adequate account of its realization must show how it is being produced in the course of man's productive activity in history. Hence a full-scale historical theory is needed. This is what Marx sets out to provide in his later work. Since Marx does not renege on his conception of the social nature of man, his historical materialism commits him to the view that the world is ripe for revolutionary socialism. He already has the idea, and the idea can only be produced in the course of man's historical productive activity, thus he needs to show how history is producing out of itself, or how men acting in history are necessarily producing, as a result of their activities, the conditions and instruments for the revolutionary overthrow of society and the establishment of socialism. But evidently what is thus realized in the course of history is nothing other than the liberation of man through the realization of his social essence.

In *Capital* the ethical doctrine of the social essence of man appears in the form of the labour theory of value, where labour is understood as essentially social labour. The labour theory of value is in the first place a theory which purports to explain what determines the proportion in which commodities can be exchanged in the market, their exchange value. Marx argues that commodities contain in them a certain quantity of a substance called value, and that this value is created by labour. The quantity of value in a commodity is the result of the expenditure in its production of so much labour. The labour that determines a commodity's value is what Marx calls homo-geneous or abstract or undifferentiated labour. Differently skilled labour is reduced to so many units of unskilled labour, so that we can talk of all labour being of the same quality, and can measure labour simply in terms of quantity. The measure of this quantity is so many units of labour time. (There are other important qualifications: that the labour is socially necessary labour; i.e. the labour actually fulfils a social demand; and that it is labour of average efficiency for that line of production in that society.)

A commodity, Marx says, is a mysterious thing. It appears to be simple, and to be determined by supply and demand. But analysis shows that the real essence of a commodity consists in the quantity of the common homogeneous substance, labour, that is congealed in it. Now Marx takes the appearance of this common substance as the essence of commodities to reveal in alien form the real underlying *social* character of labour in capitalism. He says:

A commodity is therefore a mysterious thing simply because in it the *social* character of men's labour appears to them as an objective character stamped upon the product of that labour, because the relation of the producers to the sum total of their own labour is presented to them as a *social* relation, existing not between themselves, but between the products of their labour.[31]

This Marx calls the fetishism of commodities and says that it is a consequence of the private forms in which production is carried on. He says.

Since the producers do not come into social contact with each other until they exchange their products, the *specific social character of each producer's labour* does not show itself except in the act of exchange. In other words, *the labour of the individual asserts itself as part of the labour of society*, only by means of the relations which the act of exchange establishes directly between the products, and indirectly, through them, between the producers.[32]

The relation of individual labour to social labour in these

[31] K. Marx, *Capital*, translated S. Moore and E. Aveling, vol. 1, London, 1909, pp. 42–3.
[32] ibid., pp. 43–4 (my emphasis).

passages is the same as the relation described in Marx's early work between individual productive activity and social activity. The real essence of individual labour is its social character, which is alienated in private forms of labour. This alienation of labour's social essence does not occur, Marx claims, in other forms of production. He takes first of all the case of Robinson Crusoe. Robinson Crusoe's various labour expenditures are the expenditures of one and the same person and so have a common identity which is expressed in each different mode of Robinson's labour.[33]

Marx takes the case of Robinson Crusoe because he wants to show that just as all Robinson Crusoe's individual labour expenditures are merely developments and expressions of one and the same essential labour, so also under (a) self-sufficient peasant family production and (b) socialist production, each labour expenditure by a particular person, which under capitalism appears to be private and different, but is not really so, is explicitly the development and expression of one and the same labour. The family's labour in the first case and society's labour in the second.

(a) The labour power of each individual by its very nature, operates in this case merely as a definite portion of the whole labour power of the family, and therefore the measure of the expenditure of individual labour by its duration, appears here by its very nature as a *social* character of their labour[34] [my emphasis].

(b) A community of free individuals carrying on their work with the means of production in common, in which the labour power of all the different individuals is consciously applied as the combined labour power of the community. All the characteristics of Robinson's labour are here repeated, but with this difference, that they are *social*, instead of individual[35] [my emphasis].

The direct comparison of the elements of Robinson's labour to the elements of a society's labour could not reveal more clearly the failure of Marx to allow for individuality in his conception of the relation of the part to the whole. For the family and the socialist society can only stand to the labour activity of its members in the same way as Robinson stands to the particular instances of his labour if they constitute individual identities in the same way as Robinson does, and there is *no individual self-consciousness* in their members. If the individual members were to be ends in (or for) themselves, the comparison could not hold, and the identity of the social unit could only exist through the self-conscious individuality of its members, which itself requires that individuals first constitute themselves as ends apart from the whole.

It is true for Marx, then, as it is ultimately for Hegel that the particular individual has no independent identity and existence. He is simply the expression of the life of a larger whole. He is the means to its fulfilment. This result is built into Marx's position by the naïve assumption that the particular individual is directly the social being. He has no independence, and can have no claims as an independent being. And yet this is supposed to be compatible with the view that particular individuality is fully developed!

What is unsatisfactory about the collectivist views is precisely that the particular individual must be understood only as the means whereby this higher or larger life is realized. The only entity that is an end, and that has value as such, is the whole, whether understood as the State or Society. Although it is true for Hegel that individuals have rights, as we have seen, these rights are only relative to, and thus exist as means for, the self-realization of the individuality of the State.

The individualist of Part 1 does, of course, attribute an independent existence and value to the individual as such. But by according him an objective value, by making him an end in himself in respect of his independence, and thus apart from his relations to others in a community, the individualist creates an intolerable conflict within the individual between his particular and general life. The collectivist solution to this problem of alienation, however, produces its unsatisfactory result because it operates with fundamentally the same conception of the value that is to be realized in human life. It is the objective value that is inherent in a self-determining being. Since the individualist conception, that it is the individual as such that is self-determining, and hence has value in itself, cannot be sustained, the collectivist attempts to identify the entity that has such value elsewhere, in state and society. From the point of view of realizing the inherent worth of a self-determining being in such an entity, particular individuality can appear only as the vehicle through which it is to be achieved.

To avoid these alternatives, it is necessary to abandon the idea that objective value lies in a self-determining being. What is needed is a conception of the objectivity of value that exists in the human world which is not the consequence of some wholly self-contained and self-creating being, but of the reciprocal creation of a plurality of persons whose plurality and hence separateness is not wholly absorbed in that creation. Part III is the attempt to develop such a conception.

Part III

THE RELATIVITY OF VALUE

A major element in the individualist theory which must be abandoned if a more satisfactory and coherent understanding of moral value is to be obtained is the requirement of authenticity. This is the requirement that the individual have only himself as his end in his particular life, the requirement of self-determination and the exclusion of other-determination in respect of particular life. One way of allowing another to enter into the determination of one's particular life is by choosing one's life having regard, not simply to oneself, but to another person as a valuer of that life. The value one's life has for him enters into the formation of one's choices, and he becomes co-determiner with oneself of it. The requirement of authenticity, then, would be dropped, and one would accept that the value of one's particular life is as much determined by the value it has for another as by its value for self.

Authenticity itself is a corollary of the more fundamental axiom that individuals have value in themselves. For this is the claim that individuals have value in an unmediated relation to themselves, and that the value they have for others is a consequence of the value they have in themselves. This claim must be denied, and it must be affirmed that the value of the individual for another arises in, or is the creation of, the relation that comes into existence between those particular persons. This rejection of the *absolute* value of the individual, and the affirmation of his *value in relation* to other individuals is a necessary condition of a coherent account of the possibility of morality. If we understand by morality the existence of absolute value, then no coherent account of our moral experience can be given, for there is no way within the conception of absolute value of reconciling the particular and the moral self. Whether it is the Christian or modern individualist moral view, the two will be inherently opposed *in the present*, and will demand a harmonizing solution, or salvation, in a future of this, or another, world.

It is necessary, then, to show what is involved in this proposed shift to the conception of the individual's value as a value in relation to others, and to show how much of our moral experience can be accommodated and explained by it. We must start from the individual occupying the independent standpoint. Thus I do not mean by the relativity of value some sociological view of the individual according to which he is simply the product of a social whole, and his value lies in his function in the whole. My claim will be that the social whole as a moral entity is ultimately constituted by or grounded in the individual himself in his relation to the other members of the whole. Although his particular life has value in relation to the whole, the individual is also the ground of the whole. He is both created and creator. It is for this reason that the idea of the independent standpoint as the starting point of ethical theory, and the notion of the individual's freedom that goes with it, is so important. The independent standpoint consists in the possibility of standing back from one's immersion in a particular community, in separating oneself in thought from it, and in questioning the basis of one's relation to it. In taking up this standpoint, one is denying that one is wholly constituted by one's community, and one is implicitly claiming, in raising the question of the validation of the community's claims, to participate in the ultimate determination of that validity, to be among the community's ultimate validators.

From the independent standpoint the individual necessarily sees his life as having value for himself, and raises the question of how he can come to see others' lives as having value for him. At this point the fundamental error in individualist theory is made, when, in one way or another, an objective and not a subjective interpretation is given to the individual's relation to his own life. The individual who values his own life is conceived of as requiring of others the replication of his own attitude to himself, from which the objectivist notion is derived that morality is founded in the view of persons as values in themselves. In avoiding this objectivist error in respect of the independent standpoint, we must say that from it the individual can perfectly well recognize that others are persons like himself, capable of occupying the independent standpoint and so free beings valuing their own lives, but not as such having any value for him.

What is the issue raised from the independent standpoint? The question is: given that I am an end for myself, and hence not simply a part of a larger whole, what is the basis of my relation to those others with whom I form that larger whole? One does not make substantive choices for one's life from the independent standpoint, for it is not a practical standpoint *in* life, but a theoretical standpoint from which one reflects *on* life. The answer to the question provides an understanding of the nature of one's relations to others and it is within that understanding that one subsequently makes, alters or re-affirms one's actual choices in life.

What is the non-objectivist interpretation of the ground of the value individuals have for each other? Individuals have value for each other, not because they are ends in themselves, but because they make each other their ends.[1] This is a relation between concrete individuals. Thus to make another one's end is not to acknowledge him as an end in himself, which would be merely to re-adopt the objectivist position that he is an end, because man as such is an end; it is to treat *only him* as an end.[2] At the same time it is as a concrete individual oneself that one makes him one's end. The crucial consequence of the concreteness of the persons who make each other their ends is that there cannot arise that separation between the individual's particular

[1] The apparent arbitrariness of this will be largely, but not wholly, removed in due course.

[2] Concrete individuals as ends may cover a large group, such as the British people. Furthermore, the whole of mankind can be incorporated in a system of mutual valuing to be explained later. (For the most part, however, I shall be dealing with the ethical relation as it is realized in particular political communities, and treat mankind as an afterthought.)

self and his abstract, impersonal moral self which produces the incoherence of the individualist theory. Since it is the other as this person, and not as any man, who is one's end, the value each has for the other includes his particular life.

What is it for the other to be an end for one in the non-objectivist view? As for the objectivist, the other as end is a valuer of one's particular life. But for the objectivist the other in his capacity as valuer of one is a purely abstract moral being, divorced from his own particular life. Hence when he values one's particular life, he is simply re-affirming one's own authentic self-valuation. He does not as a *concrete person with particular ends of his own* value one's particular life, and so does not value one's particular life in a relation to his own concreteness, but in relation only to his abstractness and impersonality. As particulars men must not value each other, but have only themselves as ends. Thus we have the separation and alienation between each particular life, and between particular and moral elements in each individual. For the non-objectivist, then, the other is a valuer of one's particular life, but as a concrete person, and so including his particular life. Hence he values one's particular life *in a relation to his own particular life*. To make a concrete other one's end is to adopt the following attitude to one's own life: one remains an end for oneself, that is one's particular life continues to have value for oneself and is chosen to please oneself, but, since one now treats one's particular life as a value for the concrete other also, it is chosen also to please him. In choosing a particular life for oneself, one's choice must be a life lived in a relation to the particular life of the other.

There are three levels at which one's existence for self and for other is to be understood. At the lowest or most particular level are the particular interests, particular ends or aims of individuals. These are to be formed and pursued by each individual, not having regard solely to himself, but as a value for the other as well as a value for self. This *relation* of the individual's particular interest to other particulars constitutes the second level, for it requires the joint existence of the several particulars as parts of a whole, a community. The relation between the particular interests of the members of this whole is formed by the structure of rights and duties in the community. These embody and express in substantive terms the value that particulars have for each other as members of the whole. At the third, or highest, or most abstract level is the will of the individuals who constitute the community to make each other their ends. This creates their moral existence for each other as ends, and grounds and justifies the substantive practices which form the structure of the community and through which the particular life of each member has a substantive value for the others as well as for self.

THE FUNDAMENTAL MORAL ATTITUDE

Let us begin with the third and most abstract level of this relation of self to other. It is what I call the fundamental moral attitude. It is the mutual valuation of concrete persons as valuers of each others' lives, or as ends for each other. Immediately this should be understood as specifying nothing more than that each has taken up this attitude to the other whereby he treats the other as a valuer of his life. This means only that the particular life of each individual has value for the other as well as for self, but not that any specific substantive value is thereby accorded by each to the other. It is in the first place *an attitude* of each to his own life in relation to the other. He acknowledges that the other in *association with himself*, that is through their mutual valuation as valuers of each other's lives, is the source of the value that his own particular choices for his life have. The associated will is the source of the moral value of particular choices. It creates a unity of self and other that is the common ground and justification for the particular lives of those united. In this way the other, who is co-determiner with oneself of one's particular life, is not an alien, external being, determining one from outside, but one's other self, in so far as by making him the valuer of one's life, one lives in him as well as in oneself.

In being determined in my particular life by my relation to the other, I am being determined by my other self.

This unity of self and other in the fundamental moral attitude is the condition of the possibility of morality. As has been shown in the analysis of individualist arguments in Part I, for morality to be possible the *concrete* individual must be able to treat the other's claims as in some way equivalent to his own, and to see the other as his equal. But individualist arguments fail to explain how this is possible because they insist on first allowing the concrete individual to attribute an objective value to himself, and then requiring the equivalence to be established. On my view, however, the equivalence or equality is the creation of concrete individuals adopting the moral attitude to each other, making each other their ends, and thereby creating their unified and common will.

The moral attitude of individuals to each other is essentially a common will: it creates their united or common existence, and so is the moral basis of all actual communities of men.[3] But as such it applies only between those united, or the members of a particular community. It can be said to express the truth in the modern notion of the fundamental freedom and equality of men. The equality of members of the community is given by the undifferentiated unity of self and other of the common will which grounds the whole. At this level each recognizes the other as co-creator of the whole. In regard to freedom, individuals are free in as much as they have the capacity to occupy the independent standpoint, but the freedom which is crucial to the individualist value of self-determination cannot be an attitude of the individual's particular will. In this respect he is determined by the other members of his community as well as by himself. The fundamental value of self-determination, like that of equality, is an attribute of individuals' associated or common will. It is this will which freely

[3] Of course, the common will grounding actual communities has been misconstrued as the will of God, or some objective moral will. But this is a misconstrual of the unity grounding the community. It doesn't deny that unity.

constitutes itself the undetermined ground of the value of particular lives. It is necessarily self-determining because it forms itself in the act whereby the community is grounded. But in this sense the individual can only be free by joining his will with the will of others.

The associated or common will is what underlies or grounds the substantive arrangements of a community, on the second level of related existence, as well as the worth of particular lives. It may, therefore, begin to look superficially as though it is like the pure and abstract moral will of Rousseauan or Kantian thought, especially as in the case of Rousseau we find the conception of this pure moral will as the foundation of legitimate communities. But the point about the individualist conception is that the moral will bestows value on each individual as such and hence gives equal value to the individual as a particular being, and in respect of his authentic particular self-determination. It is this conception of the value of individuals that Rousseau sees as being brought into existence among the members of a community. In my view the fundamental value of individuals that is realized in community is not a quality of individuals as such, but a quality of their associated wills. The individual apart from the community has no objective value that needs a community for its realization.

THE POSSIBILITY OF MORALITY

The question as to how morality is possible becomes in my view the question, how is it possible for the individual to come to treat a concrete other as co-determiner and valuer with oneself of one's particular life? The answer to this is that one can do so because the other is *in fact* the co-determiner of one's particular life. Hence the moral attitude is the drawing out into explicit self-consciousness of what is always implicitly there in social relations between men. For the question as to the possibility of morality raised from the independent standpoint does not presuppose that the questioner is an isolated person in a state of nature seeking others to form a society with. The question is posed for men who are already members of a particular society, and thus who already participate in relations of interdependence. Interdependence of particular lives in actual societies means that the shape and content of such lives are formed by their development within a structure of relations to others, that is a social structure. This structure necessarily places a value on particular lives in so far as they conform to it by acting out the roles specified in the structure. To say that the individual's particular life is determined by his social structure is not to say that he does not participate in his own formation as an occupant of a role in that structure, for he must acquire the capacity to direct himself in accordance with his society's values; nor does it deny the individual's capacity to manipulate, modify or change that structure to suit himself. But it is to say that, however much he himself contributes, he is also formed and determined by his place and actions in the social whole. But the whole, the social structure and its values, is, whether men think so or not, the creation of its members themselves. It is upheld only through their willing adherence to it. They may represent the whole to themselves as the creation of some God or hero, or dictated by the nature of things. But in so doing they do not withdraw their wills from the support they give to the whole: they explain only why they do support it. This conception is, of course, in my view a misrepresentation of what truly grounds the community. The other members of one's community are in fact necessarily the implicit co-determiners with oneself of one's particular worth. The basic moral attitude is, thus, implicit in actual societies, and the possibility of morality consists in the possibility of making explicit, of recognizing and developing to its full consciousness, what is implicitly true of an individual's relations to others in any scheme of social cooperation. Its possibility is inherent in the description of what it is. Ethical philosophy is not the identification and description of an ideal world set over against the world as it is, and so does not raise the question of how this ideal can possibly relate to the actual world and be realized in it. It is the description of what is.[4]

[4] This echoes Hegel's remarks in the Preface to the *Philosophy of Right*. My

It might appear to follow from the claim that morality is inherent in the human world as it is that the world is as morally good as it could possibly be, and that moral criticism of any actual social arrangements is impossible. But this absurd theory does not follow. When I say that the moral attitude is implicit in any actual society I mean that the society must constitute a scheme of cooperation through which its members contribute to and determine each other's lives. In any such scheme the full and correct moral attitude is implicit, while, of course, *some* view of what grounds the social order will have to be expressed. But the scheme of cooperation may involve roles and relations, justified no doubt in that society's own moral ideas, which from the standpoint of the full understanding of the self-conscious moral attitude may be morally unacceptable. Whether this is so or not depends on whether anything can be shown to follow in terms of substantive social arrangements from the making explicit or coming to full self-consciousness of the moral attitude. If that attitude itself requires a specific social arrangement, it can be used as the basis for criticizing other arrangements that do not meet this standard.

THE MORAL ATTITUDE AND
THE RIGHTS OF INDIVIDUALS

The fundamental moral element that is the consequence of the developed moral consciousness is the making of the other into a valuer of one's life. But the other cannot be such a valuer unless he has developed the characteristics of free personality. He must be able to control and direct himself towards the realization of purposes in his life and he must see his own life as subjectiviely a value for himself, in order to be in a position to ground the particular existence of another. Hence to have another as one's end and valuer is necessarily to treat him as a

debt to Hegel will become very clear when I describe the forms of life that the full moral attitude requires. It should be obvious however that the will that grounds ethical life in Hegel's thought is not at all the same entity as the one I describe.

person who is in charge of his own life and for whom that life is a value. The necessary conditions of so treating the other as a person involve according him certain rights, which can be called the rights of personality. These rights are the rights that individualist theory treats as the inherent rights of individuals, but they are to be understood here as rights a person is entitled to as a member of a community, and only as such.[5]

The rights of the person are rights to negative freedom on the one hand, and to welfare or well-being on the other. Firstly, the rights of negative freedom: this right involves more specifically the right not to be harmed or coerced, and a right to private property. They are, of course, rights not of the human being as such, but of the individual as member of the community. There is no right of a man as such not to be harmed or coerced, nor right to acquire property. Since they are not prior to and independent of community, they do not ground the community, but the community grounds them, and hence determines how the rights to freedom and the rights to welfare should be limited by the requirements of the whole.

The rights to negative freedom are to be justified as the necessary conditions of personality. To injure deliberately, coerce or enslave another is to deny or impair in him the basis of his personality, his being in control of his own body and mind and his directing them towards the realization of purposes for his life. But it is only in so far as one has recognized him as an end for one that one is committed not to injure the basis of his personality in this way. To attack him by these means is implicitly to deny that he has any rights as a person, and hence to deny that he is a member of one's moral community and an end for one. Such injurious acts must, therefore, be shown not to be valid in order to uphold the other's right as a member of the community. This is the primary justification for punishment, which is not to deter or reform, but to express

[5] In the following account of these rights, understood as the rights of men as members of a community, and of the forms of social life they require, my aim is only to sketch in the substantive implications of the moral attitude, not to provide an adequate elaboration.

the community's denial of validity to the injurious act and to uphold the right of the injured and hence the right of all others also. It is not necessary for this purpose that any physical penalty be imposed on the individual in so far as some other penalty could conceivably (in small and intimate communities such as families) express appropriately the severity of the community's censure. All that is necessary is that there should be an equality between the severity with which the offence is viewed by the community, and the severity of the penalty imposed on the wrongdoer.

The rights of persons not to be interfered with in the pursuit of their purposes is necessarily an equal right, and as persons men can be said to be equal. This equal right must be elaborated in a legal system which grants no individual or class of individuals a privileged position in respect of their rights as persons to pursue their purposes without interference. As in the abstract individualist formulation of these rights the right of one person is limited by the equal right of others, but in the version which abstracts rights from their ground in the community this limitation results in contradiction, since the right of one individual to realize his purposes is interfered with in so far as in fact other individuals through their prior existence and control of resources prevent him from attaining his end. By grounding the rights in community, however, the operation of the individual's right will be governed by the structure of the economic society in which it is exercised. It will be limited by the role the individual plays in that society.

The right not be coerced is hardly a controversial one, although its interpretation in the above way no doubt is. But the right of private property presents more problems. It is basically a right to the product of one's labour and the work of one's body and mind. If there is such a right, it is because what one has so produced is an embodiment of one's personality. As a person one necessarily possesses one's own powers of productive activity, one's mental and physical capacities. One cannot be a person without taking charge of them and directing them to purposes of one's own through which one gives a value to one's life. As a person one subjectively possesses these powers. To recognize the other as a person is, then, to recognize his property in these powers, his right to exclude others from interfering with them. But to justify private property in things, one needs to extend this ownership of one's own productive powers to the things which they are used to produce. The argument here is that the productive powers cannot be realized except on and through things, and that consequently the things are the necessary means through which the individual's personality is given an actual existence. To deny that the individual can have any right in the things he produces, or in the things that he needs to produce with, is to deny that the individual has any right to develop his productive powers, and hence to be a person.

There is a famous theory of man and of man's essence as consisting in his productive activity, which concludes that an individual must not sell his labour and its products to another in return for a wage. This would be to alienate one's essential human activity. This argument must be correct in so far as the alienation of one's labour is a total one, with the result that the other acquires control for the rest of one's life of one's productive powers. This would be to enslave oneself to the other, and cannot be valid, since it is a denial of one's right as a person. The fact that one has willingly enslaved oneself is irrelevant, since one cannot have a right as a person to deny one's right as a person, and hence cannot create a right in the other over oneself through the transaction. But this argument is only of great significance to us if it covers contracts of labour which give less than total control to the employer. An important feature of limited contracts may be that in alienating one's labour for a limited period one is using one's productive powers as a means to achieve some further end, as a way of obtaining money or goods which are necessary for the realization of one's more important purposes. So the question is whether it is illegitimate to use one's powers as a means to some further end. In so far as it is the realization of the end which determines one's present employment of one's powers as means, one is still in general control of the disposition of one's powers, although one delegates to the employer the immediate direction of one's activity. Yet since the employer controls and determines that part of the individual's life alienated to him, it would seem to follow that in respect of it the individual is suffering an injury to his rights as a person.

However, this conclusion depends on treating the right of the person in abstraction from community, and as inhering in the individual himself. As abstract persons each is in principle independent of the other, and seeks to give a value to his particular life that is solely self-determined. This aim is frustrated by the sale of one's labour to another. But if we see persons as realizing their rights as parts of a whole, and more specifically if we see the contracts of labour in terms of subordinate wholes, business firms and institutions, within economic society, we can treat the individual worker's relation to his firm as a partial ethical relation in which the worker does not subject himself to an alien power, since he himself helps constitute the whole which employs him. This is not, of course, intended as an answer to the Marxist view of alienated labour, since that view is not based on an individualist conception of rights at all (see Part II).

The right to private property means that an individual as member of a moral community has a right to appropriate and use whatever does not belong to others, and a right to whatever he can acquire by contract or gift. But does the right require that the individual have some property through which he can express his personality? Does it mean that quite apart from the right to welfare, the right to private property ensures his entitlement to the means through which his purposes can be realized? At this point it would be necessary to distinguish property in different types of thing, such as houses, land, tools, stocks and shares and so on, but such an investigation would take me too far away from my intention here merely to sketch in the type of social arrangement that is implicit in and required by the developed moral consciousness. So I shall say here only that the right to private property involves a right of the individual to some property in which to embody his personality. Furthermore although this is an equal right, in no way is it a right to equal things.

I have assumed in discussing the alienation of labour, that at least a right to alienate the things one owns is a consequence of the right of private property. To claim that one has no right to alienate the products of one's productive powers is to suppose that what one had so formed has become an irreversible part of one's personality; hence to alienate one's product is to alienate part of oneself. But one's personality cannot be wholly embodied in this or that particular thing nor can it be understood to require the accumulation in one's private ownership of all that has at any time served as its embodiment. The thing is only necessary for the expression of one's personality in so far as one continues to use it for one's purposes. Thus to the extent that one no longer desires so to use it, one withdraws one's personality from it, and in alienating it, one is not alienating a part of one's personality.

The right to alienate one's property involves the right to exchange it with or give it away to another. Hence the rights of contract and gift. Is there a right to bequeath one's property on death? Through a last will and testament the individual seeks the continuation of his personality after death, in so far as the recognition of his will for the thing after his death involves holding that his personality is still expressed in the thing, and hence is not an unowned thing available for anyone to appropriate. It is, of course, one's present will when alive that at a certain time in the future, on one's death, one's property shall be given to X. But how does this establish a right in X to the property when the owner is dead, since by his death his personality would seem no longer to exist and so would not be in the thing? Perhaps it is simply because we do see the personality of the dead man continuing in his things, and we do this because it is incompatible with the value we place on persons that we should treat their things as emptied of their personalities immediately on death.

This treats private property as the sole property of individuals. But if we see the property of persons as the joint property of the person and his immediate family, then the owner cannot alienate his property from the family. This would be the case if, although the individual is in law the present owner and sole administrator of his property, the members of his family have claims on his estate on death irrespective of his will in the matter. The right of the members of the family to inherit would follow directly from the fact that as members of the family they had rights in the property in any case. It is also above all in the family that the individual continues to live after his death, for, in so far as the living members respect his memory, they continue to treat him as a ground of their existence for each other as a family.

THE RIGHT TO PARTICULAR
SATISFACTION OR WELFARE

The rights of the person are in the first instance negative rights not to be interfered with in the attempt to realize one's subjective will. The other's duty in respect of these rights is to stand back and allow his will to have an effect on the world. This area of negative freedom cannot be determined solely by reference to the rights of persons themselves, for this leads to an unresolvable conflict of rights. But that there must be such an area of freedom follows from the basic moral attitude of members of a community to each other. Since included in this attitude is one's valuation of the other's particular life in a relation to one's own, it follows also that one must desire that he achieve his particular satisfaction in and through that relation. This means that one desires that the aims he sets himself as a person are realized in the relationship to oneself. One desires the other's happiness or welfare. But the desire is not that he be happy, or find his satisfaction in the attainment of his ends whatever they are. The desire is that he be happy in a place in the whole community, i.e. that whatever place he occupies he can find his particular happiness therein.

What right or rights follow from this implication of the moral attitude? The individual has a claim against others that it be possible for him to be happy in the whole. But this is not a right to be in a position to realize his authentic self-determined ends. This would be the abstract right to happiness of individuals as such apart from their membership of a whole. Since his right to happiness is held as a member of a whole, the value of his particular life is a value for others as well as for himself. Hence the value he puts on his particular life through which he seeks his happiness must be some position in the whole through which he is valued also by others. He must desire that others put the same value on his particular life as he puts on it himself, or that the two valuations are mutually adjusted and co-determined so that they tend to coincide. But he has no right that others value him at the rate at which he values himself. His right is simply that he has a particular value for them, and that his opportunities coincide with that value.

Do men have an objectively determinable value in respect of their search for satisfaction in the whole? There are relevant objective considerations here, which I will take up when considering the rights of individuals from the standpoint of the whole.

THE STANDPOINT OF THE WHOLE

The negative and positive rights of individuals described above abstractly are derivative from the mutual valuation of individuals as ends. This mutual valuing involves a unity of self and other, the creation of a common will which grounds the value for and in relation to each other of the individuals' particular lives. It is essentially the will of a community. The moral attitude comes into being as the mutual valuing of individuals as members of a community. The standpoint of the community is the basis of the rights individuals have.

It is this standpoint that distinguishes the above conception of rights from the individualist one. An individualist may well argue for the value of community, and the necessity for individuals to compromise on their rights for the sake of achieving the order and protection of communal ties. But such good sense does not show how theoretically the limitation and balancing of rights is morally acceptable. On the individualist view the individual has as much right to disregard as he has to have regard to such compromises. Hence the incoherence in the overall view of rights. But if we see that individuals have rights only as members of the whole, the standpoint of the whole is introduced as the basis of rights, and not as an additional and secondary consideration imposing limitations on them.

The standpoint of the whole is that of a unit which exists only in and through the wills of its members. As a unit it is concerned with its own survival and prosperity and this means that its members, conceiving their moral existence as members of this unit, are necessarily concerned with its survival and prosperity. The group of fundamental importance here is the self-governing political community, for it is only in this group that the self-conscious mutual valuing as ends, which constitutes the moral ground of the community, can be fully realized.[6] The self-consciousness of members of the whole as citizens in the political community requires their prior membership of subordinate wholes, in which their particular personalities can be developed and expressed. The two necessary forms of social life that must exist for this to be possible are the family and civil society.[7] The family in some form is the necessary condition of the reproduction of a community. Its modern nuclear form is determined by the nature of the individuals as developed particular personalities who unite in marriage. In this form also it prepares the children of the family for the full development and expression of their particular personalities once they set up on their own in civil society. Civil society is the economic form of the community in which the rights of persons to negative freedom and welfare are given concreteness. The separate development of civil society from the family on the one hand and the political institutions of the community on the other, and thus the full development of the particular personalities of

---

[6] But this should not be taken to exclude an international community as a community of political communities.

[7] I adopt this term from Hegel's translator.

individuals, is the necessary condition for the expression of their higher unity as citizens grounding each other's particular lives.

The family: the principle, on which the unity of the family in its members is based, is not different from that of the political community as a whole. It is the having of the other as end and valuer of one's life, which grounds each particular life in an associated will, and which means that the value of each particular life is a value for the other as well as for oneself. But the family, being a small, intimate group, cannot realize the value of the particular personality of its members adequately, for in its intimate bonds there is not the room for the development of the individual's interests that the freedom of civil society provides. The modern family is, of course, no longer the primary economic unit, so that a large part of the individual's particular activity and realization of particular values is conducted outside the family in civil society. It is obvious enough that the emergence of civil society from the family is the necessary condition of the development of personality, and consequently of the development to full explicitness of the moral attitude. As a result the unity of the family has become more dependent on the subjective factor of love and less on the objective factors of economic interdependence. Hence the unity of the family becomes more precarious, because more subject to the arbitrariness of the members' feeling for each other. On the other hand the greater intensity of the members' interest in each other's individual development increases their commitment to the relation.

But this concern in itself produces a greater freedom of the family members, especially of the children, and a lesser subordination to the authority of their parents, which leads to the easier throwing off of the family bonds. This is in part due, however, to the infection of family relations by the theories of abstract individualism, with the result that both in respect of the relations between husband and wife and in respect of the relations between parents and children the attempt is made to ensure that each individual freely develops himself without being restricted and determined by the other members of the family. This is an inherently absurd enterprise since it is obvious enough that the children, in the development of the skills brought before them in their family and society, seek and depend upon the approval of their parents. The parents determine in good part both the direction of their children's interests, and their desire to acquire particular skills. Thus implicitly, but not of course self-consciously, the value for the children of their own activities and developing skills is overwhelmingly at the same time the value these have for their parents, who are thereby the ground and determiner of the children's particular value. The attempt of parents to leave the child 'free' in the belief that one would be corrupting his will and destroying his freedom to do otherwise, undermines the confidence of the child in what is necessarily the ground of his being.[8]

The mutual determination of husband and wife is also infected by this same spirit in so far as the belief in abstract freedom and equality is imported into the conception of the marriage relation by feminist doctrines. To the extent that the woman seeks an activity outside the home, she seeks a development of personality that the man achieved only by leaving home for civil society. To deny the woman the opportunities for such self-development could be justified only if it could be shown that she was incapable of benefiting from them, or on the grounds of some higher value. While there have been those who deny that women have the capacity for personality, and indeed deny that women are properly human beings at all, the suggestion is absurd. The issue is not whether women have the potentiality to be persons and to enjoy the rights of persons in civil society, but to what extent their development in this direction is compatible with their fulfilment of a primary responsibility for the nurture of the family's children. The family is the very basis of the larger community, and without the child's initial unselfconscious identification of itself with the

[8] Like most individualist doctrines this one was invented early in the development of modern society. See Rousseau's *Emile,* and my commentary on it in *The Social Problem in the Philosophy of Rousseau,* Cambridge University Press, 1974.

small family unit, in which it is prepared for the full development of its personality in civil society and its moral nature in
political society, these latter forms of life would cease to exist.[9]
The family in its reduced and emotional form provides that care
for the development of the particular individual as a value for
himself within a confident unity with others and so value for
them, that enables him to enter into the apparent anarchy of
civil society, find his way there, and become a citizen.

How these contrary requirements might be satisfactorily
resolved I do not propose to consider, but the importation into
the discussion of them of the feminist ideology involves a mis-
conception of the unity of the family. Feminism has no doubt
contributed to the freeing of women from their subordination to
patriarchal conceptions of their role, just as individualist theories
of the freedom and equality of man have contributed to the
development of civil society, personality and the self-governing
political community. Nevertheless, feminism, like individualism
generally, conceives of unity in terms of the equal freedom of
independent persons.[10] It is quite unable to reconcile the conflicting claims of husband and wife to freedom within the family,
and is quite incapable of justifying the different roles of the two
as parts of a whole which they themselves through their associated will constitute. It is this latter conception that must be justified in some way if the family community is to exist and flourish.

Apart from the abandonment of false conceptions of the
ground of the relation between the family members, nothing
would so help the family as an increase in, or the avoidance of
any further weakening of, the objective interdependence of the
members. This would make the subjective attitude of love for
the others as their other selves more firmly grounded in an
exchange of services, a differentiated contribution to the survival and prosperity of the group in and through which the
members find the conditions of their own flourishing. Of course

---

[9] I do not mean that there would cease to be governments, and economies,
I mean rather that the specific forms of these in which the moral nature
of man is fully developed would cease to exist.

[10] This refers to liberal or individualist feminism. There is, of course, a
socialist feminism.

at this point we come up against a very old modern attitude, which sees marriage as a restriction and impediment to a true or pure love, pure in the sense that it is the unconstrained, self-determining will of each to remain with the other, in relation to which the marriage form imposes an institutional commitment and legal and material consequences which impair the lovers' freedom. But this idiocy is arrived at by treating the moral attitude, which grounds the relations between members of a community, as independent of the material objective inter-dependence, and as having to be so in order that relations between persons can be governed by nothing but the pure moral love of the other. The love must be unconstrained by material interest, as if the men and women were not necessarily particular beings, and as if their relations were not relations of inter-dependence of such beings.

Civil society: On growing up the child 'leaves' his family so to speak and seeks an independent position in civil society. He seeks the development and realization of his particular needs, interests and purposes. Civil society is the whole in which both the rights of the person and the rights to particular satisfaction are to be satisfied. What is civil society? It is an economy in which individuals are involved in the production and exchange of goods and services of all kinds. The individual is to be understood as in the first instance engaging in such productive and exchange activities with a view to realizing ends and aims of his own to his particular satisfaction. This is a central dimension of his activity in this sphere. But the economy is such that he cannot attain his ends except through cooperation with others, by associating with them in production or by exchanging goods and services. Each is dependent on the others for the attainment of his ends. The economy as a whole consists in the first instance of these relations of interdependence by which each attains his end only through his dependence on the others. Each is and must remain self-directing, i.e. have a conception of what he wants for himself, and have the opportunity and freedom to engage in activity directed to the satisfaction of those wants.

Since each can gain his end only through providing something which will contribute to the satisfaction of another, each is means to the other's ends, and hence we can say that each is necessary to the other, completes the other's life in so far as it is directed to an end. This arrangement by which each is part of and so completes the existence of the other is dependent on the whole system; the more prosperous the whole, the more prosperous the parts will be, and conversely. Individuals' activities are parts of a whole system of relations, and they achieve their value as parts of this whole system.

If each attains his end only through the others and hence through his participation in the whole, it would seem right and proper to concentrate on the standpoint of the whole and view the parts from that standpoint. The primary aim would be the prosperity of the national economy, and one would view the parts as contributing to that end. It would, then, be natural enough to interpret this as a collectivist socialist standpoint according to which the national economy is a vast extended family in which the particular activities of the individual are seen as the carrying out of the common enterprise, the joint family effort, while his satisfaction is to be found in the success of the whole with which he immediately identifies himself.

This is not an entirely false picture of the individual's proper relation to the national economy. The trouble is, however, that if we understand the collective unit to be correspondingly collectively organized and directed from the centre, that is planned and determined from the standpoint of the whole, and not through the self-concerned decisions of particular individuals, there can be no rights of the person, and no negative freedom. The individual cannot take any decisions on his own as to what activities he will seek to engage in and develop himself in. The decision as to what is to be produced and carried on is a decision of the central authority, or that of a delegated authority within a more general plan of the central agency. The objection to this from the standpoint of ethics is not the economic inefficiency of such a system but its denial of the right of personality, and hence the undermining of the possibility of the explicit actualization of the moral standpoint since this requires the self-conscious apprehension by members of the community that they are the ground of the values of the organized community.

Collectivist socialism, of course, claims to be the realization of the ideal of the self-governing community. But while in conception the central economic authority is supposed to be an expression of the common will of the associated workers, it cannot make effective the representative political institutions necessary to give reality to that conception, precisely because it denies its members the rights of persons and negative freedom in civil society. Another way of putting this is to say that collectivist socialism fails to separate civil society and political institutions; indeed as we have seen in Marx's thought it prides itself on overcoming this distinction and uniting economic and political man. The crucial point is that if the individual in association with others is to be seen as the ground of value, then it must be the case that he is capable of taking up the independent standpoint and is, therefore, an end for himself. He must be free in the sense of being able to conceive of a plan for his life, and direct himself towards its realization. But he could not come to think of himself in these terms, unless his being an end for himself in thought is explicitly separated from his feeling of unity with his actual group. He must alienate himself from his group in order to arrive at this grasp of his freedom and personality, and in order subsequently to be able to reintegrate himself with his group, in accepting his dependence on and formation by it, on the basis of his participation in the common will. Thus a 'family' conception of the relation of the individual to his group could not produce this alienation and reintegration. For the alienation is precisely alienation from an immediate identity with one's group. The spirit of collectivist socialism denies that this alienation is necessary, and hence in its actual socio-economic organization must deny the individual any freedom to conceive of his particular ends apart from the whole.

The *separate* organization of the economy has as its fundamental requirement the opportunity for the individual to think of his particular ends in the first instance apart from the whole. He must be able to think of his particular life as an end for himself, and hence of himself as the ground of the value in his life; for only then can he see how his value for himself can be realized in dependence on others, through which each contributes to the particular existence and value of others. He can then understand how he can be both a part of a larger whole and at the same time the ground of the whole. The separate organization of the economy makes the development of particular personality possible, and thus makes possible also the political realm in which the underlying unity of individuals as members and ground of the whole is expressed.

This personal liberty, or negative freedom, in civil society does not involve the readoption of the classical liberal scheme of individual rights limited only by the equal rights of others understood as the right to appropriate privately and so on. The free market economy is only arrived at if we treat the rights of persons in abstraction from the standpoint of the whole, and we treat the whole as 'looked after' only by an invisible hand. The impossibility of the liberal position consists in the fact that it cannot accommodate the dependence of the particular individual on other individuals, the fact that he is not solely self-determined, but determined as part of a larger whole. The individual must accommodate himself to this and cannot do so if his right is understood abstractly as residing in him apart from his relations. Thus what has to be combined in civil society is, on the one hand, the attitude of the individual in which he can think of his life apart from the whole, and, on the other hand, the attitude in which he sees his life determined and completed by others as parts of a whole. The first element is satisfied in so far as the individual has the opportunity to make decisions regarding his own particular life, choose his occupation and engage in activities by himself or with others. These activities must not harm others, but harm is defined not in terms of abstract rights, but in terms of the rights of individuals as members of the existing socio-economic system. Within the existing structure of rights one has the right to pursue one's own good for oneself, being required to think of others only negatively. One has the opportunity of determining one's own particular life as one thinks fit, and hence has oneself as one's end. But one determines one's particular value within the larger structure and through cooperation with others, so that the other side of one's choice is the value put on one's particular activities by others within the whole. Hence what one is, is determined through and by others and the whole. The value for oneself of one's particular life is at the same time value for the other established in the network of relations in civil society. This value of one's particular life as value for the other is ultimately acceptable to one because both one's own and the other's life are parts of a whole structure of values which is grounded in a unity of self and other.

I do not mean by this that there is bound to be a harmony between the value the individual sets on his particular life and the value it has for others. There may well be a deep conflict between these valuations, a conflict that cannot satisfactorily be resolved, and which leads to the disintegration of the relevant association. Such conflicts do not involve, however, the same incoherent opposition between the individual's particular and general life as in individualist theory. For in the above account the individual's desires for his own life are not values for others because, as expressions of the value of self-determining individuals, they are values in themselves. Consequently they are not values for others independently of any relation to the particular lives of others. Since in my account each values the other's particular life in a relation to his own, there is no right of the individual to the satisfaction of whatever he authentically conceives as his purpose. But this does not mean, on the other hand, that the individual whose ambitions are not satisfied in his existing relations must simply conform himself to his opportunities. Each must choose for himself whether to seek to realize himself in his existing relations, or to change or dissolve them.

Civil society is not just a set of individuals related in a market supported by a legal system that defines the rights and duties of individuals. Individuals are members of groups and associations of various kinds, which have a partial ethical nature. These are business firms, trade unions, professional associations, universities, and indeed any association of men sharing a common interest from pigeon fanciers to opera lovers. An understanding of their partial ethical nature and the individual's relation to them can be approached through the distinction made by Michael Oakeshott between two modes of association, the enterprise and civil modes.[11] An association in respect of the enterprise mode is a 'relationship in terms of the pursuit of some common purpose, some substantive condition of things to be jointly procured, or some common interest to be continuously satisfied'.[12] The association exists solely for the realization of the common purpose, and its organization and the relations between its members are defined in its terms. An association in respect of the civil mode, on the other hand, is an association not defined by any common purpose, or substantive aim, but by moral conditions; however, moral conditions are such that they do not prescribe any substantive outcome, but only the terms on which relations between participants should be carried on. They are formal rules, and the members of the association are united solely in respect of their adherence to the rules.

Oakeshott in fact draws this distinction between the two modes of association too sharply, and as a result cannot present a convincing account of the civil mode. However, the distinction is useful for understanding the difference between civil society and political community. The too sharp distinction consists in the attempt to identify the civil mode as a pure relation without any substantive purpose. Translated into my categories it would be an association in which men recognize each other as ends for each other, this recognition being expressed in a system of institutions and rules that would be wholly neutral in respect of the different members' particular interests and values. The ethico-political terms of the association define merely a set of non-discriminatory, formal rules within which members pursue

[11] M. Oakeshott, *On Human Conduct*, Clarendon Press, 1975, pp. 114 f.
[12] ibid., p. 122.

their particular satisfactions by themselves or in cooperation or association with each other. This conception falls into the error of trying to separate off the moral or common dimension of the lives of individuals from their particular value, so that each can determine the latter by himself, since the rules of the general association are supposed to be neutral between all such values; while at the general level each is a pure end for the other, having no particular nature and value in respect of that relation.

Nevertheless an association in civil society has only a partial ethical nature and is not a political community precisely because, as Oakeshott says, it is wholly constituted by the substantive aims that define its character. As a result the other members of the association are ends for the individual only in relation to that purpose. They are ends for the individual to the extent that they are at the same time means for him to realize his end. They are thus only partial ends for him; they are not the ultimate ground, in unity with the individual himself, of the whole extent of the individual's particular worth. In an ethical community the other as valuer of one's particular life is not as such a means to one's own particular ends, but the ground of the worth of all one's particular ends. It is this fundamental aspect of the ethical community that Oakeshott separates off from the determination of substantive values. But the ethical community cannot avoid having a substantive character of some kind in its choice of a particular ordering of substantive values. However, it is not defined by any particular ordering, and indeed its freedom consists in its *self-determination* in this respect. An enterprise association does not determine its ordering of values, which is given to it by the specific purposes common to its members.

Individuals must be free to join and leave enterprise associations as they please provided that they meet the requirements or possess the qualifications laid down by the association. In the case of economic enterprises the common purpose is to make a living through association in the production or supply of goods or services, and membership of such associations must be governed by this overriding aim. The particular form such enterprises take, whether capitalist or cooperative, can to some extent be regulated by law, but not to the extent of excluding the negative freedom of individuals to associate in whatever way they please, so long as they do not injure the rights of others. Thus individuals must always have the right to form capitalist or cooperative enterprises, even if the law encourages the development of some intermediate form.

In the pursuit of particular interest individuals engage in types of activity through which they make a living by fulfilling a function in the national economy. On the basis of such groupings of individuals, particular associations of common interests are formed. But the members of civil society also form very broad groupings known as classes. Classes are based in the first place on the occupational structure that the modern economy requires. This structure consists in an order of occupations from high to low with professional, managerial and administrative occupations at the top end and unskilled workers at the bottom. A broad distinction is traditionally made between workers by hand, skilled and unskilled, the absurdly called working class, and workers by brain, the managers, administrators etc. But class is constituted by more than the occupational order. It involves the association of broad occupational functions with substantive social identities expressed in particular styles of life and orderings of values. Necessary for the emergence of the class identity of ranks in the occupational structure is the fact that it is whole families which have positions within the structure, and that individuals partly acquire the identity of a particular rank through their membership of the family.

The individual's opportunities to develop himself in civil society will, of course, be determined by his particular family and class background. Given an initial differentiation of classes justified as above in terms of the needs of civil society as a whole, children born to those in superior positions will have better chances of acquiring the skills that will enable them in their turn to attain these superior positions than children born to those in inferior positions. The major factor producing this inequality of opportunity will be, in the first instance, the home background, for it is this that ensures that a public educational system not designed to favour children from the higher classes will nevertheless be used to greater advantage by the latter. Thus, while there would be no legal restrictions on individuals from any class from entering any occupation, in practice class inequalities would remain. The degree of inequality of opportunity will depend primarily on the degree of inequality of condition that exists between the classes in the first place. But in discussions of the principle of equality of opportunity it is assumed that justice requires the equalization of the opportunities of individuals from all classes to attain the superior positions in civil and political society, as though the inequality of class condition and equality of opportunity were compatible.

According to the doctrine of equality of opportunity, as formulated in Williams's influential article,[18] a limited good, e.g. access to superior positions, should be allocated on grounds which enable individuals from all sections of society to have an equal chance of satisfying them. But this requirement makes it clear immediately that the environments which govern individuals' chances must be the same for the children of each section of society. This means either that the inequality of condition between the classes must be removed, or that children must be removed from their families and brought up in state nurseries. But the first alternative is incoherent, since it involves the proposal to abolish classes as a means of making opportunities for entering them equal for all. The second involves the destruction of the family and hence the destruction of the necessary condition for the development of the free personality for the sake of promoting the equal opportunity of each to develop himself. One way out of the unsatisfactoriness of trying to conceive of equality of opportunity in terms of opportunities for individuals to attain superior positions in society is to re-define what the equal opportunities are opportunities for. They are not opportunities to engage in a competition for scarce positions, but opportunities to participate in the common

---

[18] B. Williams, 'The Idea of Equality' in P. Laslett and W. Runciman (eds.), *Politics, Philosophy and Society II*, Basil Blackwell, 1962.

life of a community.[14] But it would seem that the good here is not a limited one, and hence that opportunities to enjoy it do not have to be allocated on any grounds at all. It can be made available to all. The idea of equality of opportunity is, then, irrelevant.

The doctrine of equality of opportunity is obviously the product of individualist theorizing, and its unsatisfactoriness ultimately derives from the incoherence of that position. It treats the individual in respect of his opportunities in civil society as though he should stand entirely on his own as a value in himself. Since all such individuals must be of equal value, it is unacceptable that one individual should have greater opportunities than another simply because of his particular location in the world. But the individual does not stand on his own and is not a value in himself. His value for others exists as a member of a community, and this community is in the first instance the family. He enters the world as a value in his family, and hence necessarily enjoys whatever benefits this position provides him with. Whether this is just or not depends on the justice of the general social arrangements which establish differentiated social conditions, and not on the position of the individual children. If the differentiated environments between the classes in the social whole is a fair one, then the unequal opportunities for the children of different classes resulting from this situation must be fair too, and the principle of equality of opportunity must be understood to operate on the basis of such differences.

As discussed above the individual as an end for the other members of his community has a right to his particular satisfaction, and this means that he has a right within civil society to a sphere of activity in which he can find his satisfaction. This is provided for in so far as the individual fulfils a function in some group in civil society and attains a standard of living that is fair in terms of the general social arrangements. Of course, particular persons may be dissatisfied with their position

---

[14] J. Schaar, 'Equality of Opportunity and Beyond' in J. Roland Pennock and J. Chapman (eds.), *Equality: Nomos* IX, Atherton Press, 1967.

in the whole. But the right to particular satisfaction is not a right to any position that one desires; it is only a right to some activity in which satisfaction is possible. Whether one's individual position in the social whole is unjust or not, as distinguished from the position of one's group, depends on whether other people with inferior talents and abilities have been preferred to one in one's desired field of activity. The right to particular satisfaction does, however, require policies against unemployment and the provision of welfare services to remedy poverty and destitution. Civil society, as Hegel says, having torn the individual from his first family and so deprived him of the welfare to be found in the more primitive extended forms of the family, must turn itself into a kind of second family for the individual, and provide public educational and welfare services which enable him to fulfil himself in a particular activity within the whole, and to attain a degree of satisfaction that must be relative to the general standard of living in the community.[15]

In civil society the individual in pursuit of his own good engages in activities which contribute to the functioning of the economy as a whole. Thus there is a standpoint of the whole in civil society, which involves concern for the good of the whole or the prosperity and expansion of the economy, and of the parts as contributing to that good. But civil society cannot be organized so as to pursue that good directly without denying the rights of particular individuality. Hence the good of the whole must be pursued indirectly through the decisions of individuals and groups concerned with their own ends. The good of the whole must be represented by a framework of general laws and institutions within which individuals and groups must operate. But since the members of civil society are not as such concerned with the general good, this concern must be separately organized and pursued, in other words in political society. As a member of civil society the individual legitimately sees the general structure of laws and institutions as that

[15] G. W. F. Hegel, *Philosophy of Right*, edited by T. M. Knox, Clarendon Press, 1952, paragraphs 238–45.

through which he can attain his own ends. But he has to accept the general structure as a limit on his actions, and, since this gives other members claims against him, he has to respect them as ends for him in the very act of using his relation to them as means to his own interests. Because the individual is not conceived here abstractly as an end in himself, and because consequently he sees his particular interests as essentially mediated through the lives of others and the whole, and hence as valid only in a relation to them and the whole, he can accept these limits on his action without incoherence. He conceives his particular interests in a structured relation to the interests of others, so that he accepts the value of others for him in pursuing his own interests.

Political society: The standpoint of the whole, which is implicit in civil society, but cannot be realized within civil society without the destruction of the essential character of that society, is separately developed in the institutions of political society in the state. As members of political society individuals are citizens and their only legitimate concern is the common good. This good is expressed internally in a structure of general laws and institutions which regulate the activity of individuals and groups in civil society, and also determine the position of the family and its members. Externally the common good concerns the position of the community in relation to other communities.

The laws are the general terms on which individuals' particular interests are to be related. Their essential character is that they are *general* rules. Thus they must not be concerned to determine what individuals' particular interests are to be, but only the structure within which individuals decide for themselves. The requirement of generality does not, however, involve the belief that there exists the possibility of a wholly neutral structure of laws which expresses the equal value of each individual. The general rules and practices adopted will necessarily be the product of a balancing of different interests and of the values they represent in civil society. Hence the laws cannot be said to be neutral in respect of these different interests.

Yet this does not mean that there is no such thing as the standpoint of the whole, and that instead of a common good there exists only a public arena in which conflicts of interest are fought out. This picture of political society contains, of course, an element of the truth, but the suggestion that it contains the whole truth is utterly destructive of community. Once the groups of civil society come to think in these terms, political society will soon be at an end. The standpoint of the whole involves the consideration of the claims of the different interests of civil society with a view to maintaining or altering the balance of the laws and institutions from the point of view, not of this or that interest, but of a conception of the long-run interest of the community as a whole in its environment, its prosperity and success. Just as the individual develops himself as a free being in forming a conception of his life in terms of an ordering of values to be realized in it, so also must the community form a conception of its long-term identity in terms of an ordering of values that it seeks to realize. The determination of the specific balance of the laws is at the same time the expression of the community's self-conception. It is by forming itself in accordance with such a self-conception that a community achieves its self-determination. The institutions of political society are the forms through which this freedom is realized.

One cannot understand the community's self-determining will, therefore, as simply a majority will of the conflicting interests, since that majority will can have as such no authority to speak for the whole by expressing the community's self-conception. The standpoint of the whole is not a sectional self-interest, even if this section is a majority; it is rather a balancing of such sections in a conception of an ordered life. It must include a legitimate place for all sections and the values they embody.

At any one time the community's existing arrangements will represent a more or less coherent self-conception and most attempts to change the laws will have to appeal to elements in that identity which, it will be argued, are not adequately reflected in the legal position of this or that group. Political debate will thus be carried on for the most part in accordance with the conservative understanding of politics as the pursuit of the intimations of a tradition of behaviour.[16] But it is always open to individuals and groups to challenge the community's traditional self-understanding and seek to bring about a new ordering of substantive values.

Nothing in this idea of a substantive ordering of sectional interests in a system of laws and institutions should be taken to alter the account given above of the basic rights that structure civil society. The balancing of interests cannot be such as to eliminate the rights of particular individuality to negative freedom and welfare. These rights are the bedrock of civil society, and their preservation ensures that the laws must be general. The balancing of interests involves rather the specific determination of the content of those rights, without which, as argued above, the rights can only be conceived abstractly and cannot in themselves constitute a system of organized law. For example, one cannot from the abstract consideration of the right to private property and contract determine what the respective rights and duties of landlords and tenants should be. The specific determination of the law regarding tenancies must involve a judgement as to the place to be given in the ordered life of the community to these two sections. Yet there are limits to what can be so decided, given on the one hand by the requirement to preserve the effective property right of the landlord on the other by the desirability, having regard to the right to welfare, of giving the tenant some security.

The generality of the laws consists in the fact that only types of activity are covered in the laws and not individuals and types of individuals e.g. classes or races. This requirement does not ensure that the laws will not be tyrannical and oppressive, since types of activity may be forbidden or so restricted as to deny to some sections of the community a reasonable means of self-expression. Within these requirements the various sections of the com-

---

[16] For such an account see M. Oakeshott, *Rationalism in Politics*, Methuen, 1962, especially the essay on Political Education.

munity may each fight with such intensity to achieve dominance for its own conception of the community that the free organization of civil and political society will be destroyed, or the existence of the community as a single entity will be ended.

The system of laws and institutions which are determined within political society and which govern civil society express the value that members of the community as individuals and as members of sectional groups and associations have for each other. Thus in voting for a general structure of laws citizens are voting for a conception of the community as a whole in which its parts are ordered in a certain way and have a certain value in relation to each other. This will be true also of the institutions that determine the character of political society. Obviously, the character of the political constitution will determine the sorts of decisions made in respect of the organization of interests in civil society.

Can one say anything about the form the political constitution must take in order to realize the idea of the community as a whole expressing itself through its political institutions, whereby its members give actuality and specific content to the value they have for each other? I shall limit myself here to a brief consideration of the representation of the people in political society. Since the order of the community expresses, not a will that is grounded in some external source, a God or Eternal Law, but in the associated will of the community's individual members, the members, as a whole or in any part, cannot be treated as a subject element, whose role is simply to conform themselves to the externally ordained order, but must participate in the determination and expression of the community's order. They must all be members of political society, that is to say they must have rights as citizens. In any large state, then, the character of political society must be determined in large part by the requirement of representative institutions. But what sort of representation is appropriate? The so-called liberal democracies have developed representation in the apparently individualist form of one man one vote, where the ideal seems to be to realize as far as possible the equal value each individual has as an end in himself. It is for this reason that Hegel, from whose account of the forms of ethical life I have borrowed greatly, argues against this type of representation and for the representation of individuals, not as individuals, but as members of the classes and corporations of civil society. This argument, however, reveals the fact that the ultimate ground of the community for Hegel does not lie in the associated wills of its members expressing the value they have for each other, but in an absolutely free will that needs particular men as the vehicle for its self-realization. On my view the ultimate ground is constituted by a collection of specific *individuals* valuing each other as ends for each other, and hence members of the community must have rights in political society as individuals; but not, of course, as abstract individuals who are *independent* values; rather as individuals whose value consists in their common will and mutual valuing. Thus representative institutions based on the votes of individuals are to be understood as the way in which this grounding of the community in the common will of its associated members is given expression.

The representation of individuals in political society should nevertheless not be interpreted to mean that the effective value of these votes must be made as equal as possible. For the aim is not to give actuality to the value that each person has in himself, but to realize a conception of an ordered whole in which the individual's mutual valuing is expressed. Thus it is absolutely necessary that the various sections of civil society should be brought into a relation to the institutions of political society, and individuals as such cannot do this. This necessary function can be provided for, however, not by giving representation directly to the sections, but through the political parties. The parties can be understood as coalitions of interests organized with a view to realizing a conception of the proper identity of the community as a whole. A party must not be based on a single class, but must have to persuade voters from all sections of society to support it in order to be able to win political power. In so far as this is the case individuals will be represented in political society through the mediating organ of a party which embodies and expresses an ordered conception of the whole. Party is the central mediating agency whereby the apparently abstract individualist conception of one man one vote is overcome, and the individual as citizen is related to a substantive order. The flourishing and competition of at least two broadly based parties is, thus, necessary to the flexible working of a political society in which all are to be citizens and express their commitment to and creation of the whole, and yet be present there not as independent individuals, but integrated as members of the whole. Of course, the parties must not be in too extreme an opposition, for, in that case, the change of government from one party to the other will lead to radical alterations in the community's self-conception, which must result in incoherence and conflict. There is no institutional arrangement that can ensure against this, and the self-determining life of communities, as that of individuals, is inherently exposed to breakdown and disintegration from within.

ETHICAL CRITICISM

Ethical criticism of what exists is thus possible on the basis of the rights that men should have as members of particular communities, namely those rights described in the above sketch of the necessary implications of the moral idea.[17] As I have said above, this gap between the ethical ideal and reality can only be a partial and not a thoroughgoing one. The ethical idea is necessarily firmly grounded in actual relations between men, which must contain and express at least primitive forms of ethical life. The full form is implicit in these more primitive forms, and when the implications of ethical life are understood, criticism of its inadequate actualization becomes possible.

The non-existence of civil and political rights is a familiar enough basis of ethical criticism, but of more interest perhaps is criticism which is concerned, not with fundamental rights in

---

[17] The sketch is not intended to cover all the rights that men should have, and I have not mentioned the rights of assembly, of free speech and so on necessary for a free political society.

an obvious way, but with the way in which rights are given determinate specification in a community's ordering of values. There may be cultural minorities within the community that identify themselves in terms of membership of some other community because of their shared national or cultural identity, or who wish to constitute themselves a self-determining community. Here the criticism may not be that the minority are denied civil or political rights, but that these rights are so circumscribed by the context within which they have to be exercised, namely the choices of the dominant group, that there is no or insufficient scope for the expression of their own particular self-conception. The criticism cannot, of course, be that the larger community has some substantive self-conception expressed in its general arrangements, since it cannot be a self-determining unit without such a conception. So the criticism must be that this self-conception is developed in such a way as not to be generous enough to the desires for self-expression of the minorities within it. This again must involve a balance of interests. The toleration of minority cultures cannot be such that it undermines altogether the sense of an identity shared by the whole, since this would be the destruction of the community as a self-determining unit. So the community as a whole is entitled to put limits on what it will tolerate for a minority within its general scheme. Yet should the minority find those limits unsatisfactory to it, a crisis in its self-conception must ensue. It must either accommodate itself to the dominant culture, or it must seek to establish its independence or association with another community considered to be more congenial.

There, thus, arises the question of the rights of cultural groups, the so-called nations, to be self-governing. Just as there are no objective rights of individuals as such, but only rights of persons as members of a whole on the one hand, and on the other the subjective 'right' of each to treat himself as his own end, so there are no objective rights of nations to be free, rights which existing communities are required to recognize. The 'rights' of peoples are rights to be subjectively ends for themselves, i.e. to conceive themselves as a whole, and seek to realize their life together as a self-governing unit. Nations do not have, any more than individuals, worth as such. They have subjective worth in so far as they conceive themselves as a collective unit. But if their subjective self-conception comes into conflict with the subjective self-conception of other groups, a separation or accommodation has to be made. The conflict is ultimately about the possession of the territory inhabited by the opposed groups. Thus, if the minority simply seeks to emigrate en masse to some other territory, it cannot rightfully be interfered with by the dominant group, however much the quality and quantity of its members may be missed. If a man or a body of men can find somewhere else to go, he or they must be entitled to withdraw his or their will from the existing community and associate with others.

The original community affirms its original identity to be embodied in a certain territory, which is the property of the whole.[18] It cannot passively sit by while minorities within it set themselves up upon its territory as independent, self-governing units. Or rather, it may do so, if it feels that it is sufficiently strong within smaller bonds, more cohesive and effective without troublesome minorities. But this is a *decision* the original community must make. The decision not to yield involves the attempt to coerce the minority into acceptance of their present identity, or of some modification of it, while for the minority the decision is to seek its independence by force of arms. Here there are no clear criteria of right and wrong; it is certainly not the case that every community suppressing a minority rebellion is in the wrong. Here we have a quarrel in the world in which men must take sides, and stake their futures, and the futures of their children and peoples, and in which individuals and groups must decide who and what they are to be.

---

[18] This does not contradict the right of private property, since that right is held by individuals only as members of the whole. At the same time this right cannot be withdrawn.

SUBJECTIVITY AND OBJECTIVITY IN MORALS

On my view there are no objective moral values in the sense that men are required by the constitution of the world to govern their conduct in terms of these values. Men and nations may choose to be pure egoists and reject moral life entirely. Moral value is grounded subjectively in the associated wills of individuals (or nations) who as members of a community (or community of nations) recognize each other as ends. But there are two kinds of objective factors which limit this subjectivism and perhaps make it more palatable. In the first place, as I have argued above, the moral attitude is necessarily implicit in relations between men who are interdependent. It follows from this that men who are objectively, i.e. as a material fact, interdependent, have no right to, and cannot adopt as a general practice, the attitude of egoists to each other, while they continue in the same state. Wrong is the denial that another, on whom one is in fact dependent, and so who is implicitly an end for one and ground and determiner of one's life, is such an end and has any claims on one at all. Since the other is, as implicitly the ground of one's being, one's other self, to deny him is to deny that self, and hence is a form of self-denial.

To deny that the other in a relation of interdependence has any claims on one is to affirm that one's own will is the only one that has value in the relation, and thus involves the attempt to coerce the other into yielding what is necessary to the completion of one's own existence without returning anything to him. It is the attempt to make another a tool of one's will. Slavery is coercion of this kind in which the master seeks to be morally independent of those on whom he is materially dependent.

The slave is a thing and not a person for the master, because the master does not treat him in the relation as an end for himself, and thus as subjectively a person capable of choosing and controlling his own life. To treat him as an end for himself in the relation would be to treat him as seeking to realize ends for himself in and through the relation, and thus as a valuer of the master's life in a relation to his own. This would be to treat him as, together with the master, grounding their particular lives in their associated wills. Thus the master cannot recognize the slave as even subjectively a person and continue to deny him rights. To see that on which one is dependent as a person is to see that one's own existence is in fact mediated through the other. Note that my argument here is not the same as a typical Kantian argument which produces the same result. For the Kantian, a person is a being of objective worth, and one must treat him as an end for one because he is an end in himself. My claim is that a person is a being of subjective worth, and that this is sufficient to yield the conclusion that slavery is objectively wrong. It is not a matter of choice as to whether one treats another on whom one is dependent as an end for one or not. It is an implicit commitment of one's will arising from one's own conception of persons as subjectively grounds of value together with the relation of dependence on another subjective will.

The fundamental element in right and wrong is the affirmation or denial of the personality of the other in one's relations with him. Besides coercion, deceit and fraud are attempts to obtain from the other his contribution to one's existence, while avoiding a fair return on one's part. It is to use the other purely as a means to one's own existence and to deny that he has any claims in the relation. In the case of deceit, however, one pretends to recognize the claims of the other while effectively depriving him of their substance.

While right is the recognition of the claims of the other in one's relations with him, goodness is the positive desire that the other flourish in these relations, and, corresponding with that, evil is the desire that the other not flourish but suffer harm. The aim is to make oneself the cause of the other's flourishing or suffering. The good will takes for granted that the other is a person for one and an end in one's relations, and so has right-claims on one, while it actively seeks the other's fulfilment in the relation. In evil one recognizes the other as subjectively a person, since one desires his non-flourishing, not as an animal, but as a conscious, purposive being. Evil is the recognition and not the denial of personality in the other, but it is the recognition of personality as a negative value for one, as something to be frustrated and harmed. By one's very evil will towards another, one is treating the other as an end for one. One seeks a relation to him by which one can have an effect on his life; hence one's own life is a value in relation to his life. He grounds one's life, since part of the meaning of one's life lies in its effect on the other, and thus on the other's valuation of it. One is necessarily treating him as a value for one at the very moment at which one is trying to destroy that value. Evil is then a self-destruction, since, in destroying the other, one is destroying that which gives one life.

The objectivity of morals as described above consists in the necessity for those already in relations of dependence to adopt the moral attitude. The moral attitude is in such circumstances not a matter of choice, because it is already implicit in one's relations to the other, and hence in explicitly rejecting it, while continuing in those relations, one puts oneself in contradiction with oneself in the person of the other being. Moral sub-jectivism, however, is often taken to involve a belief that, while some sort of morality may be necessary, there is no universally valid or objective set of moral values. My argument above rejects this form of subjectivism also, since I claim that the moral attitude must be expressed in certain specific social forms, namely a nuclear family, a civil society containing the rights of persons to negative freedom, and a self-governing political society with representative institutions. To say that the moral attitude objectively requires these social forms is to say that it is most fully expressed in them. Thus it is not to claim that other social forms exist which are wholly devoid of the moral attitude. It is to claim that these forms as expressions of the moral attitude are deficient. This deficiency generally, but I do not think necessarily, involves a deficient understanding of the moral attitude itself. This is true in the contemporary world in the case of communist social forms which are based on the con-fusions in Marx's ethical theory. In respect of social forms of earlier ages, we are dealing with arrangements that express a very different conception of the ground of morality, namely one centred outside man. In this work I have taken for granted the superiority of the modern conception: on that basis the requirements of the moral attitude are determined and are not a matter of arbitrary choice.

Thus the element of subjectivity in my conception of morality lies in the non-necessity of entering into moral–social relations with others and in the choice of those with whom one will enter into such relations. This choice is for most people one which exists in principle only, namely which community one wishes to be a member of, and whether one wishes to withdraw from social relations and seek a hermitage in some wild spot where one can be self-sustaining and independent and hence outside morality altogether. This ultimate subjectivity has, however, no doubt been of more importance in relations between independent communities, than in relations among individuals.

Two independent and self-sufficient communities may be in competition for scarce resources. Since they are not in relations of dependence, they are not ends for each other, but exist in a Hobbesian state of nature. It follows on my view that each is entitled to seize the goods and territory of the other, and destroy its members, since morality cannot be brought to bear on the relation. This situation can only be overcome if they enter into a system of relations whereby they accept each other as ends, and thereby abandon the egoist attitude. But this change cannot, of course, be said to be morally required, and the reasoning leading up to it cannot be other than an ultimately arbitrary choice of one way of life over another.[19]

THE UNITY OF THE HUMAN RACE

This subjectivism makes it possible to deny the moral unity of the human race. Since belief in this unity has formed part of

---

[19] There would be losses in such a moralization of relations, e.g. the loss of a certain wild and noble heroism expressed in the life of tribes that feel free to rob and kill each other.

our moral education, although hardly of our practice, for a long time, its denial is no doubt an offence to our sensibilities. But my position only makes its denial possible; it is equally possible to affirm it, and indeed in so far as we live already in an inter-dependent world our options in this respect are removed. If the moral unity of men is to be affirmed, it can hardly be expressed through the creation of a political community, as described above, that includes the whole of mankind. The com-munity of mankind must be a community of political com-munities. It is as members of particular states that we affirm our moral unity with the rest of mankind as members of other states. This should not be taken to require the political division of the world as it exists at present. In the affirmation of one's unity with the members of other states is the desire that they flourish in some political community related to one's own, but not necessarily in those communities in which they are presently to be found.

But there is another sense in which the moral unity of the human race can be affirmed. In adopting the independent standpoint and seeing oneself as an end for oneself, one must see other men as capable of adopting the same standpoint and of being such ends. In recognizing the subjective personality of all men, one is recognizing in them a capacity for constituting with oneself a moral community. Mankind exists as this potentiality for moral unity.

INDEX

alienation,
    in Feuerbach, 140
    in Hegel, 117, 123
    in Marx, 117, 142–5, 149, 153
        5, 6, 8, 55, 179
altruism, 35, 37–8, 45, 51, 54, 57, 85
associations, particular, 182–3
authenticity, 21–4, 107–8, 157

Barry, B., 112n
benevolence, 22, 24, 51–4
Benn, S. I., 30–3, 36, 44
Bentham, J., 87, 90, 91

classes, 184
common good, 188–9
common ownership, 100, 104
common will, 162, 172
community, standpoint of, 172–93
    family, 174–7
    civil society, 177–88
    political society, 188–93
Conservatism, 190

desires, I and non-I, 24–5, 36–7, 41
Dumont, L., 23–4
Dunn, J., 40n
Dworkin, R., 13, 14, 20, 35n, 114n

economic theory, classical, 23–4
egalitarianism, 96, 101, 102–9, 110
egoism, 22–5, 36–7, 39, 41–51, 55,
    81, 84–5, 111, 114
equality,
    of individuals, see under indi-
        viduals, equal value of
    of opportunity, 34, 184–6
    of particular natures, 26–7
    of rights, see under rights
ethical criticism, 193–5

evil, 197–8

feminism, 176
Feuerbach, L., 138–41, 144, 146–50
Flathman, R., 4n, 16n
freedom
    and equality, connexion of, 11–14,
        26
    liberal theory of, 96–102
    negative, 102, 106, 114, 166,
        178–80, 190
    in Hegel, 119–22
    in Kant, 75–8
    of agents, 6–8, 27–32, 34–5

game theory, 47–8
Gauthier, D., 46n, 47n, 49n
Gewirth, A., 27–30, 33, 44, 61n, 85
God, as ground of moral order, 2, 3,
    22, 99
goodness, 197–8

happiness, 15, 87, 89–91, 171–2
Hare, R. M., 112n
Hart, H. L. A., 17n
Hegel, G. W. F., 1, 80, 138, 164n,
    173n, 192
    alienation, 117, 123
    civil society, 129–30, 187
    dialectic, 121–3
    ethical life, 127–8
    family, 128–9
    free will, 119–22
    indiviuality, particular, 117, 123,
        128, 131–5, 154–5
    infinite spirit, 118
    personality, 123–4, 129
    state, 130–1
Hobbes, T., 7, 40, 110, 115

Index

egoism, 22, 23, 39, 41–51, 111,
114
  equal liberty, 44–5
  natural law, 42–6, 48, 49
  sovereign, 48, 50
  state of nature, 8, 9, 41
Hume, D., 52

independent standpoint, 5, 6, 8, 9,
19, 25, 26, 36, 55, 60, 158–9
individual
  as end for himself, 7, 19, 26, 60–2,
85, 154, 158–60, 179–80
  as end in himself, 19, 23, 61–2,
74–5, 85, 154, 159
  concrete, 159–62
  pure, 11, 18, 29, 31, 73, 83, 160
individualism, 4, 18, 19, 21, 25–6,
39, 45, 63–4, 115, 117, 157
individuality, particular, 117, 123,
  in Feuerbach, 139–42
  in Hegel, 117, 123, 128, 131–5,
154–5
  in Marx, 117, 137–8, 146–8, 154–5
individuals, equal value of, 1, 11–19,
25–38, 45, 67, 73, 82–3, 86, 94,
104, 108, 114
interest, relation of private and
common, 50–1, 56, 67, 82,
136–7

Kant, I., 3, 7, 34, 40, 115, 119
  freedom, proof of, 75–8
  goodwill, 69–70
  individual, as end in himself, 74–5,
197
  nature, 79–80
  pure practical reason, 70–1, 75
  rationalism, 39, 64, 69–81, 118
  theoretical reason, 76–7
  universalization, 71–4

laws, generality of, 188–9
Letwin, S., 4n
Locke, J., 3, 4, 8, 23, 97–9, 101
life, right to, 16
Lukes, S., 17–18, 35n

Mackie, J. L., 49n, 72

Mandeville, B., 23
mankind, unity of, 199–200
Marx, K., 1, 198
  alienation, 117, 140, 142–5, 149,
153
  history, 151
  individuality, particular, 117,
137–8, 146–8, 154–5
  individualism, critique of, 68–9n,
135–8
  labour theory of value, 151–3
  man as species being, 137–8, 142,
143
  relation to Feuerbach, 138, 143–4,
146–51
  socialist production, 145, 153–4
Mill, J. S., 88, 91–3
Miller, D., 15, 103
minorities, 194–5
morality
  fundamental standpoint of, 161–3
  possibility of, 5, 38–41, 51–2, 55,
63, 81, 157, 162–5
  relativity of, 157–61
  secondary principles of, 20, 87,
95–6
  and self-interest, 81–6, 109–14
  subjectivity and objectivity in,
196–9

Nagel, T., 38–9, 53
nations, rights of, 194–5
needs, 15, 102–3
Nozick, R., 12, 35n, 97–9, 101

Oakeshott, M., 182–3, 190n

Pareto-criterion, 106–7, 114
Pocock, J. G. A., 40
political parties, 192–3
political representation, 191–2
private appropriation, 97–102
promising, 43, 71–2
punishment, 166–7

rationalism, 19, 36, 39, 40, 54, 57,
69–81, 84, 118
Rawls, J., 8, 9, 15n, 35n, 73n, 106n,
109–15

Index

reasons for action, 29–30, 36
Rees, J., 35n
rights
  equality of, 12–16, 96–109, 167
  of animals, 16
  human, 12, 15, 17
  primacy of, in modern moral view
    2–4
rights of individuals as members of a
    community, 165–93
  as citizens, 191–3
  of personality, 165–9, 178–9
  of private property, 169
  of welfare, 171–2
Rousseau, J. J., 39, 40, 108n, 110,
    115, 163, 175n
  citizens, 57, 66–8
  conscience, 57, 65
  Emile, 62–6
  equality, 62–4, 67
  general will, 66–8
  natural goodness, 55, 60n, 65
  natural man, 57–9
  pity, 55, 59, 63–4
  private and moral will, opposition
    between, 66, 68
  social corruption, 55, 57, 59–62,
    65–6

Schaar, J., 186n
self
  and other, unity of, 161–2

divided, 57, 81–6, 118
  moral, standpoint of, 96, 102,
    104–5, 108–9, 112–13, 115
  particular standpoint of, 102, 108,
    110, 114–15
self-interest, see under egoism
Skinner, Q., 40n
slavery, 196–7
Smart, J. J. C., 17n, 90n
Smith, A., 23
socialism, collectivist, 179
state of nature, 8, 9, 57–9, 199
sympathy, 37, 39, 40, 51–5, 57, 64,
    81, 84–5

Tawney, R. H., 35n
Taylor, A. E., 46n

universalization, 71–4, 85
utilitarianism, 3, 7, 86–95

Vlastos, G., 35n

Warrender, H., 45n
welfare, right to, 16–17, 171–2, 190
will, particular and moral, 20–3, 66,
    68, 82–4, 102
Williams, B., 17n, 24, 33–6, 40n, 44,
    90n, 185n
Wilson, J., 35n
wrong, 196–7

CAMBRIDGE STUDIES IN
THE HISTORY AND THEORY OF POLITICS

Editors: Maurice Cowling, G. R. Elton, E. Kedourie, J. R. Pole, J. G. A. Pocock and Walter Ullmann.

A series in two parts, studies and original texts. The studies are original works on political history and political philosophy while the texts are modern, critical editions of major texts in political thought. The titles include:

TEXTS

Liberty, Equality, Fraternity, by James Fitzjames Stephen, edited with an introduction and notes by R. J. White

Vladimir Akimov on the Dilemmas of Russian Marxism 1895–1903, An English edition of 'A Short History of the Social Democratic Movement in Russia' and 'The Second Congress of the Russian Social Democratic Labour Party', with an introduction and notes by Jonathan Frankel

J. G. Herder on Social and Political Culture, translated, edited and with an introduction by F. M. Barnard

The Limits of State Action, by Wilhelm von Humboldt, edited with an introduction and notes by J. W. Burrow

Kant's Political Writings, edited with an introduction and notes by Hans Reiss; translated by H. B. Nisbet

Karl Marx's Critique of Hegel's 'Philosophy of Right', edited with an introduction and notes by Joseph O'Malley; translated by Annette Jolin and Joseph O'Malley

Lord Salisbury on Politics. A Selection from His Articles in 'The Quarterly Review' 1860–1883, edited by Paul Smith

Francogallia, by François Hotman. Latin text edited by Ralph E. Giesey. English translation by J. H. M. Salmon

The Political Writings of Leibniz, edited and translated by Patrick Riley

Turgot on Progress, Sociology and Economics: A Philosophical Review of the Successive Advances of the Human Mind on Universal History. Reflections on the Formation and Distribution of Wealth, edited, translated and introduced by Ronald L. Meek

Texts concerning the Revolt of the Netherlands, edited with an introduction by E. H. Kossman and A. F. Mellink

Regicide and Revolution: Speeches at the Trial of Louis XVI, edited with an introduction by Michael Walzer; translated by Marian Rothstein

George Wilhelm Friedrich Hegel: Lectures on the Philosophy of World

History: Reason in History, translated from the German edition of Johannes Hoffmeister by H. B. Nisbet and with an introduction by Duncan Forbes

A Machiavellian Treatise by Stephen Gardiner, edited and translated by Peter S. Donaldson

The Political Works of James Harrington, edited by J. G. A. Pocock

Selected Writings of August Cieszkowski, edited and translated with an introductory essay by André Liebich

STUDIES

1867: Disraeli, Gladstone and Revolution: The Passing of the Second Reform Bill, by Maurice Cowling

The Social and Political Thought of Karl Marx, by Shlomo Avineri

Idealism, Politics and History: Sources of Hegelian Thought, by George Armstrong Kelly

The Impact of Labour 1920–1924: The Beginnings of Modern British Politics, by Maurice Cowling

Alienation: Marx's Conception of Man in Capitalist Society, by Bertell Ollman

The Politics of Reform 1884, by Andrew Jones

Hegel's Theory of the Modern State, by Shlomo Avineri

Jean Bodin and the Rise of Absolutist Theory, by Julian H. Franklin

The Social Problem in the Philosophy of Rousseau, by John Charvet

The Impact of Hitler: British Politics and British Policy 1933–1940 by Maurice Cowling

Social Science and the Ignoble Savages, by Ronald L. Meek

Freedom and Independence: A Study of the Political Ideas of Hegel's 'Phenomenology of Mind', by Judith Shklar

In the Anglo-Arab Labyrinth: The McMahon-Husayn Correspondence and Its Interpretations 1914–1939, by Elie Kedourie

The Liberal Mind 1914–1929, by Michael Bentley

Political Philosophy and Rhetoric: A Study of the Origins of American Party Politics, by John Zvesper

Revolution Principles: The Politics of Party 1689–1720, by J. P. Kenyon

John Locke and the Theory of Sovereignty: Mixed Monarchy and the Right of Resistance in the Political Thought of the English Revolution, by Julian H. Franklin

Adam Smith's Politics: An Essay in Historiographic Revision, by Donald Winch

Lloyd George's Secretariat, by John Turner

The Tragedy of Enlightenment: An Essay on the Frankfurt School, by Paul Connerton

Religion and Public Doctrine in Modern England, by Maurice Cowling